Freezer Bag Cooking:
Trail Food Made Simple

By Sarah Svien Kirkconnell
http://www.freezerbagcooking.com/

Bay Street Publishing

A Division of Bay Street Communications, LLC

Freezer Bag Cooking: Trail Food Made Simple, 1.06

Published by Bay Street Publishing, a part of Bay Street Communications, LLC.

Other Information:
Additional writing and editing by Matthew Kirkconnell
Additional editing by Mona Ching

Cover Design by Debbi Murray of DrrtyGrrl Designs
http://www.drrtygrrl.com/

Cover photography Copyright © 2006, Matthew Kirkconnell
http://www.baystreetphotos.com/

ISBN-10: 1-4116-6031-5
ISBN-13: 978-1-4116-6031-1

To Kirk, thank you for encouraging me to go after my goals and dreams and for being there with me every step of the way.

To my son Ford, who has been my hiking partner since his first steps.

To my friend and hiking partner Tori, thank you for encouraging me to go farther with this idea, start the FBC website, and for not letting me forget about my grand idea of eating ramen every day on The Wonderland Trail.

Preface

In the fall of 2004, my hiking partner Tori and I got to talking and realized we needed to broaden our food assortment on the trail and come up with more recipes of our own. While we had heard about outdoor cooking in freezer bags on internet forums and dabbled in this a bit, we wondered how we could improve the method and, in the course of our discovery, help others with more than just occasional posts on outdoor-focused internet forums.

We set out a challenge for each other: on each day hike, backpacking or car camping trip, each had to show up with a recipe. The on-site preparation rules were simple: a stove, a tea kettle or small pot, a freezer bag with the meal and a spoon were all that could be used. I started borrowing some lightweight cooking gear from my boyfriend Kirk (now my husband), eventually getting some of my own, and since then Tori and I have never looked back. I created the Freezer Bag Cooking™ web site to house all of our creations and others that were submitted to me. The idea for this book and the recipes herein came out of that web site and discussions with others.

I hope you enjoy the book!
Sarah

Introduction

What is Freezer Bag Cooking™?

Freezer Bag Cooking™ (FBC) is a style of outdoor cooking and set of techniques that simplify the outdoor eating experience to its essentials, without sacrificing food that tastes good.

At it simplest level, FBC involves preparing a meal at home by placing the ingredients into an ordinary zip top freezer bag. When ready to eat, you cook the meal by pouring water (usually boiled) into the bag and letting it simmer in a cozy (see Gear and Techniques chapter). Once ready, you can eat the meal right out of the bag with cleanup amounting to licking your utensil and closing the bag.

To some though, Freezer Bag Cooking™ and this book are more of a style than just a collection of recipes (someone even coined the term "FBC style" on a web forum). Many people have started using this style of cooking on every outdoor trip, regardless of activity. So while you may try the recipes by themselves, you might find that you like the cooking style more and more and transform the rest of your outdoor menu to adapt to the FBC style. You can get as fancy as you like or keep your meals simple. The style lends itself to a variety of foods and tastes; some covered in the FBC books, some on our web site and some not yet dreamed up. Perhaps you will even create your own FBC style recipes. If you discover any good ones, please let us know!

Contents:

Introduction   v

Gear & Techniques   1

Breakfast   9

Drinks   15

Salads & Vegetables   22

Soups   30

Lunch   37

Dinner   42

    Rice   43

    Couscous   59

    Pasta   65

    Wraps & Burritos   73

    Stuffing, Potatoes & Everything Else   77

Desserts   83

Index   90

Techniques & Gear

Eating well doesn't mean you need to carry a big kitchen with you on the trail. You don't need to carry heavy pans, multiple pans, a lot of fuel or have to do much cleanup after your meals. You can eat great food, enjoy a nice variety of meals, and be done eating before dark. There are a few items and techniques that will go a long way to achieving edible nirvana…or as close as one can get.

The basic techniques of Freezer Bag Cooking™:

Whether you create your own or use the recipes in the book or website, they usually end up in freezer bags. Once you have the meal in the bag and you are ready to eat, the basic tasks when ready to "cook" your meal are easy. Bring water to a near boil (only takes 3-4 minutes for the amounts you will need), measure out what you need into a cup and then add the correct amount to your freezer bag. This way you avoid painful burns, adding too much water, or touching your freezer bag with a burning hot piece of metal and melting the bag. Use common sense when dealing with hot items!!!!

Mix well, gently squeeze all the air out of the bag, zip it shut and wrap in a pot cozy, more of those later. Then let sit for 5-15 minutes, stir well and enjoy.

Tools needed (the basics)

- **A backpacking teakettle or lightweight pot with lid.** It should hold around 2 1/2 cups of water. While most any metal will work well, it is best to look for aluminum or if you can afford it, titanium.

- **An outdoor stove.** We prefer a canister style or alcohol stove.

- **A windscreen to go around the stove.** You can make them from a turkey pan, household stove liner pan or heavy duty foil folded 3 times. This will dramatically increase fuel efficiency. They can be bought commercially as well.

- **A spoon or GSI Foon™.** For stirring and eating. No overly pointy sporks or any forks! Holes in the bag are bad.

- **A Lexan mug/cup.** Get one with measuring markers on the side. It can double as your drinking vessel and measuring cup for water.

- **A box of good quality freezer bags.** (See section on bags).

- **A permanent black magic marker.** You will use this to write on bags.

- **A cozy.** While optional, it is highly recommended for keeping your food warm while the boiling water does its magic. (See section on cozies)

Bags

Look for good quality zip top freezer bags for most things. My personal favorites are the Glad® brand bags that are a greenish blue color. Ziploc® brand is another excellent choice as well, but most any brand of freezer bag will do fine. You can use the little snack bags and sandwich bags for certain side ingredients that need to be kept separate from the main meal.

If you can find them, the best freezer bags are the ones that are pleated on the bottom and can stand on their own. One of the big makers came out with them a few years back, but they have all but disappeared off store shelves for some reason. If you find a good source for these mythical beasts, let us know.

I do recommend bringing 1 or 2 extra bags with you on trips, especially if you are taking sharp pointy ingredients like dried pasta.

While no one I know has ever had any bad occurrences on the trail using freezer bags (i.e. "leakers", blowouts, etc.) there is a small chance of it occurring. So make sure you pay attention, set the bag in front of you as you pour the water, be careful when pouring the boiling water and don't do it in your lap. Use common sense in cooking in camp, just like you would at home.

As far as cleaning and reusing the bags, do NOT reuse ones that have held anything near boiling water. Sometimes it jeopardizes the outside seals, especially on cheaper bags. Otherwise you can just wash them out with soap and hot water. If you want to put them into the dish washer, make sure they are wide open and use a clothes pin or something to affix the bag to a tine of the dishwasher rack.

If you squeeze or knead your bags to mix up the food, be very careful. Be sure to push out all of the air before you do this. The steam from the hot liquid can cause a buildup and your kneading could cause the bag to pop open. Having your meal unexpectedly plop in your lap is not a good experience.

Cozies

A cozy is a container in which you put your bag of food inside to insulate so your food rehydrates properly. If you have ever prepared a commercial freeze-dried meal, the instructions have you put the food bag in the foil bag after mixing in the boiling water. A cozy serves much the same purpose.

There are commercial cozies available from many sources, like the ones I make myself and sell on my web site (www.freezerbagcooking.com), but there are others if you search the Internet. You can also use a number of items to make your own cozy. You can use a fleece jacket, a hat, or whatever extra clothing you have lying around (Though if you are a true light backpacker, you don't have a lot of extra clothing lying around!) In areas where bears are prevalent, do NOT use your clothing!! If you want to make your own dedicated cozy, you can use anything from two potholders sewn together, neoprene, Reflectivix, a homemade fleece pouch or a pipe insulator cover (the kind you might use outside on a faucet to insulate it in the winter). A winter spigot insulator is one the best cozies you can make for winter and cold temperature use. It is bulky, but worth the space in my opinion. You can fit your gear into it in your backpack, and it holds a quart freezer bag perfectly when cooking. Plus, it holds it upright, so you have a "bowl" for eating. This makes for less mess and easier eating. Spigot covers can be found at your local hardware store or online.

Ingredients

Wondering what something is? Can you use something similar? Where can you expect to find this product?

Building your outdoor pantry at home:

I always keep on hand at home the following items:

> Instant Rice
> Couscous
> Instant refried beans
> Instant hummus mix
> Cheese sauce powder
> Dried minced onions
> Dried veggie mix
> Dried Bell Peppers
> Dried Tomatoes, flaked
> Dried Mushrooms
> Soup mixes, such as brands as Cup of Soup®, Lipton® and Knorr®.
> Gravy packets
> Stuffing mix
> Pouches or cans of tuna, salmon, cans of chicken, turkey and hamburger.
> Ramen pouches or dried pasta

I hunt for and keep around an assortment of condiment packets containing honey, ketchup, salt, pepper, mayonnaise, etc. Whenever I eat out, go for coffee or what have you, I always ask for extra packets. If you prefer not to forage for packets or you are looking for something unique, an excellent source for most any single serving item is Minimus (www.minimus.biz).

Things with Protein:

Canned chicken can usually be found in 3 oz, 5 oz and 10 oz sizes. I prefer the 5 oz size for meals for 2. Make sure you do not drain off the broth in the can as it has good flavor for the meals. Be sure to get the cans with pull tops. You can also find chicken in 7 oz foil pouches. They are great to feed 1 starving or 2 sharing adults.

Ham can be found in some geographic areas, usually in 7 oz foil pouches. You can sometimes find it in small cans, but only get pull-tabs or pop top style. Do not confuse this item with a certain canned Hormel product.

Tuna is probably the most common to find and comes in foil pouches. The 3 oz size is perfect for one person and the 7 oz size for two. Albacore is the better choice, in my opinion. If you are doing long days, use the oil-packed version. Tuna steaks are now available in pouches too.

Salmon, while pricier than tuna, has more body and is not as fragrant as tuna usually. It does have more fat in it and less protein, but if you need to get oil in your diet, it is better. Salmon also works better in cream soups and chowders. The small pouches are great for 1 person. Larger pouches are good for 2 persons. Canned salmon can be used, just make sure it is bone and skin free.

Sometimes you can find shrimp, clams, crab or other seafood in small pouches and they are all good! Just abide by the "best before" dating.

Hamburger can be found in some geographic areas in pouches, though I would strongly recommend avoiding the temptation in this case. It is just as easy to cook it at home and then dehydrate it yourself, with better results.

TVP or Textured Vegetable Protein is a great meat substitute. It is readily available in most bulk food sections and can be used by itself or for adding a little thickness to most any meal, even ones that already have meat. If adding TVP to a recipe, be sure to add an equal amount of water, otherwise your meal might be extra thick.

As for Spam®, Vienna sausages, cocktail wieners and other potted meat products…stay away…stay very far away!!!!

Vegetables and the Like:

Hummus is made from garbanzo beans (sometimes known as chickpeas) and spices. Instant hummus is a powder you mix with cold water to make a spread. It can usually be found in the natural or ethnic section of grocery stores usually. It is a good source of protein and tastes great with flat bread. Fantastic Foods makes the best mix. You can also make your own and dry it.

Instant refried beans (Flakes) come in brown or black bean and can be found in bulk in grocery stores and natural food stores. Sometimes you have to use more water than the box calls for to get a proper consistency. You can also find it sold as "bean soup" mixes, but can be used to make refried beans.

Veggie flake/dried veggie/freeze-dried veggie mixes are a mix of shreds of dried vegetables, which usually includes a variety of different vegetables. It can be found in the bulk sections of grocery stores or natural food stores. It is sometimes sold as "Soup Starter". You can also find this online through some retailers. Another option is to make your own by dehydrating a 16 oz bag of frozen mixed veggies. Make sure to chop them up into smaller pieces, if they are not already so, before putting them in your dehydrator. When dry, pulse them in a food processor or blender to the point where they are flakes so they rehydrate better. The "Cadillac" of vegetables and my personal favorite, are the Just Veggies brand of freeze-dried vegetables. They are a little on the pricey side, but they are fantastic and rehydrate perfectly. Check out the Just Veggies (www.justtomatoes.com) web site. Also check out Harmony House Foods (http://www.harmonyhousefoods.com). We are finding other brands of freeze-dried veggies in the baby food section of grocery stores.

Dried mushrooms come in a few varieties, but personally, I like good plain white mushrooms for recipes.

Dried bell pepper flakes can usually be found in green or red, rehydrate quite fast and bring flavor to the party. They can be purchased at some natural food stores, spice and herb stores, as well as online.

Dried onions are very straightforward and can be found in most grocery store, bulk food outlets. Make sure to get the containers with the smaller pieces as some places carry two sizes.

Dried tomatoes/powder can be found in bulk herb sections and gourmet sections. If you cannot find powder, you can run tomato pieces thru a mill, coffee grinder or food processor. You can also dry tomato paste in a dehydrator and powder it. Freeze-dried versions are also available.

Dried carrots can be found online, in spice and herb stores and sometimes in natural food stores. To make your own, cut them in chunks or strips, dry them, then pulse a few times in the blender or food processor. Another idea is to use a vegetable peeler to make carrot shavings. Dried carrots from Just Veggies or Harmony House Foods are also great!

Various Powders and Other Items:

Instant milk powder comes in non-fat milk is widely found, whole milk (Nido) and can be found online or in gourmet cooking stores in the baking area. Powdered soy milk can be used in most recipes as a replacement.

Soy milk powder can be found in your grocery stores in the health food section or bulk food aisle in some stores. 2 Tbsp powder will usually make 8 oz of liquid, so if you prefer to use soy, substitute 2 Tbsp of soy for every 1/3 cup dairy milk powder called for in a recipe. Most times it is much higher in protein than dairy. A good brand to look for is Better Than Milk.

Freeze-dried fruit can be found labeled as a variety of thing either in the cereal aisle or more recently in the baby food aisle. Sometimes they can be found as "Cereal Toppers." Just Veggies makes great freeze-dried fruits.

Coconut cream powder is a high fat/calorie powder that makes coconut cream. It's sort of an odd item, but really adds a nice taste and texture to foods. It can be found online, in Asian food stores and in some Asian sections in your local grocery store. It is best used in curry dishes to make them creamier. It is sold on our web site www.freezerbagcooking.com.

Cheese sauce powder, like from a mac-n-cheese box, can be found in the bulk food section at many grocery stores. Any traditional recipe that would normally call for melted cheese can be turned into backpacking food with this item.

Low sodium chicken bouillon is the best you can find! It has NO MSG!! It makes for a great base for a lot of recipes. If you use it though, you may need to add a pinch of salt to your food. This sounds odd, but at least this way you can control how much MSG and salt are in the dish. The brand of bouillon I use is Herb Ox.

Instant rice is best bought in bulk - most any brand will do. In any rice recipe you can use instant brown rice instead or in combination. Tip: I always add a tablespoon extra rice to any meal in a freezer bag I make, as sometimes instant rice can be a tad soupy.

Couscous is tiny pasta, full of protein and carbs and comes in different flavors. It needs only water added to it, so it works well warm or cold. Couscous has a lot more protein than most rice, so it makes an excellent base for many meals. Look for the plain or whole wheat varieties. It can be found at grocery and natural food stores near the rice mixes or in the bulk section. Any time a recipe calls for rice, you can usually substitute couscous. You may have to play around with how much water the recipe needs, if you substitute.

Sodium Content and Healthy Eating

Some of the recipes in this book contain ingredients that are a little high in sodium, specifically the soup mixes. For most people, the slightly elevated amount of sodium is fine and if they are exerting themselves, they probably need it. If you are one of the unlucky few, like myself, for whom sodium causes issues, find alternative ingredients or mixes or simply steer clear of these recipes. Also, there are some recipes in this book, but a lot more on the web site, that are marked as "low sodium".

Also, some of the recipes in the book are down right not good for you. Most of the recipes have a good balance of the foods we need when we're outdoors and exercising, but every so often you want something a bit more decadent. Some are just so good, we had to include them. The forthcoming second book in the FBC series will have a much healthier selection of food, I promise.

What to always carry with you in your outdoor "kitchen":

The good thing about freezer bag cooking is that your food is prepped ahead of time and ready to go, but the drawback is that you never know how your taste buds are going to feel that day. So carry with you in a small snack baggie with the following items:

> A couple of salt and pepper packets from a fast food restaurant.
> A couple packets of parmesan cheese.

I keep around a couple snack size baggies with some herbs/spices such as thyme, garlic, dried parsley, etc. If you are planning on making soups in a freezer bag, carry some instant mashed potatoes or TVP to use as a thickening agent in case you mess up a little and add too much water (not that I have ever done that!) If you are making a lot of rice or couscous dishes carry a little extra, in case the meal comes out too thin. You could add about 2-3 packets of parmesan cheese to help thicken most meals.

Whenever I want to perk up a recipe, I use:

For savory meals try one or more of the following items: dried thyme, garlic, dried parsley, fresh ground black pepper, dried chives, dried rosemary. I love using "Pizza Blend" and "Spaghetti Blend" herbs, sold by Tone®, and also in bulk. They add intense flavor with sometimes little to no salt.

For desserts and breakfasts I use cinnamon, ginger, nutmeg, pumpkin spice blend or pie spice blend. A favorite item for me is candied ginger. If you buy it in bulk, it is very affordable. Dice it up very fine and add it to your oatmeal for some zing.

General Questions

The "How do I eat out of the bag" question:

This can take a little practice, but after your food is ready, roll the top 1/3 of the bag down (imagine you are rolling you sleeves). This will make your bag into its own bowl. A long handled spoon works best. If eating soup or chowders, pour it into a mug or put the back into something like a Fozzil® bowl.

The "How do I feed two people" question:

Many of the recipes listed are written to feed two people, which might make one wonder, how do you feed two out of one bag? My answer to this has been to bring an extra bag with you (usually reused from having held a dry food before). After the meal is ready, I do the final stirring, and then divide the meal between the two bags.

Not into freezer bags, but you want to use the recipes?

If you don't want to use freezer bags, you can make your meals by adding the dry ingredients directly into your boiling water, in the pan. Other options would be to use an insulated mug, use Glad Ware®, Rubbermaid Take-A-Longs® or similar food containers that have a lid. If it is dishwasher safe, it is a pretty good bet you can use it. These can be put in soft-sided cozies too.

Other Information

For more information, tons more recipes, FBC related articles and to purchase some of the gear mentioned in this book, visit my web site at http://www.freezerbagcooking.com/. If you have any questions, FBC related stories and photos, please email me at sarah@freezerbagcooking.com. I'd love to hear from you.

Breakfast

Breakfast on the trail can mean many things to many people. Some like to wake early, eat light and get going. Others like to sleep in, waiting for the sun to fill the landscape, have a long lazy morning and/or eat a bigger meal. My favorite is right at dawn, as the sun just starts to show itself, when the mountain peaks are beginning to glow. There is something magic about that time. No one else is awake usually. Just my hot beverage and me standing alone in the wilderness. This is one of the main reasons I backpack. A primal statement that I can survive the night in the wilderness. You know the day will bring more adventure, but for now it is just your time.

Regardless of your preferences, what you need is food to get you moving and warms you up. Food that tastes good, drinks you want to savor and whether you want to admit it or not, fuels your body until your next meal.

Fruity Morning Couscous

In a quart freezer bag put:

1 cup couscous
1 handful dried fruit (raisins, dried cranberries, apples, peaches, coconut, etc - diced)

Take brown sugar in a separate bag.

In camp: Add 2 cups boiling water to the bag and stir well. Put in a cozy for 10 minutes, fluff and top with brown sugar to taste.

Yield: Serves 2

Breakfast Trail Rice

In a quart freezer bag put:

1/2 cup instant rice
1/2 cup powdered milk
1/2 cup chopped dried fruit
A small handful of chopped walnuts or pecans
2 1/2 Tbsp brown sugar
1/2 tsp ground cinnamon
Salt to taste (optional)

In camp: Add 1 cup of near boiling water, stir well and put in a cozy for 10 minutes.

Yield: Serves 1-2

Breakfast Ramen

1 block any flavor ramen (save flavor packet for another day)
Small bag of brown sugar
Pinch of cinnamon
1 handful of raisins or dried fruit
1 handful of nuts

At home: In a sandwich bag, mix the nuts, cinnamon and brown sugar. Put the ramen, raisins and/or dried fruit in a freezer bag.

In camp: Add 1 1/2 cups boiling water to ramen bag. Put in cozy for 5 minutes; drain off most of the water. Put in sugar, cinnamon and nut mixture to taste.

Yield: Serves 1

Trail Oatmeal

In a quart freezer bag put:

2 packets instant oatmeal, your choice of flavor
2 Tbsp dry milk, powdered soy milk or protein powder
2 Tbsp dried fruit

In camp: Add 1 cup boiling water. Stir well, put in cozy for 3 minutes. Let cool a bit and eat.

Yield: Serves 1

CyndiH's Super Oatmeal

In a quart freezer bag put:

2 packages instant oatmeal
1 Tbsp dry milk
2 Tbsp brown sugar
1 Tbsp each: dried cranberries, chopped dates & chopped almonds.

In camp: Add 1 cup boiling water, stir and let sit till cool enough to eat.

Yield: Serves 1

Cinnamon & Sugar Couscous

In a quart freezer bag put:

1/4 cup couscous
2 Tbsp dry milk or powdered soy milk (plain or vanilla)
1 Tbsp brown sugar
1/2 tsp cinnamon
Pinch of salt
1-2 Tbsp chopped almonds

In camp: Add 1/4 - 1/2 cup boiling water (add lower amount for drier couscous). Put in a cozy for 5 minutes, stir well and eat.

Yield: Serves 1

Fruit & Nut Breakfast Couscous

In a quart freezer bag put:

1/2 cup couscous
1/2 cup dry milk
1/4 cup dried cherries
1/4 cup finely chopped walnuts
3 Tbsp brown sugar
1/2 tsp cinnamon
1/4 tsp salt

In camp: Add 1 1/4 cups boiling water stir and put in cozy for 10 minutes.

Yield: Serves 2 (this recipe can be halved for 1)

Morning Trail Grits

In a quart freezer bag put:

3/4 cup instant grits (Two, 1oz servings)
1 Tbsp bacon bits
2 tsp butter powder
1/4 tsp granulated garlic
1-2 Tbsp powdered cheese mix

In camp: Add 1 cup boiling water and stir well. Put in cozy for 5 minutes and stir again.

Yield: Serves 1

Morning Mountain Wraps

Mountain House's freeze-dried scrambled eggs are recommended. Make sure you buy the instant type!

1 package freeze-dried eggs, plain or fancy.
4 soft taco size tortillas
2-4 packets salsa
(Optional) 1-2 oz of your favorite cheese

Prepare the eggs, being careful with the amount of water called for. Let sit. Check to see if any water needs to be drained. Put cheese on the tortillas, spread the eggs on top, put on salsa, roll up and eat.

This is also very good with shelf stable crumbled bacon added.

Note: If I am with friends that don't rise early, this is an awesome breakfast to make. It is also a great choice if you have children with you. For a change, use strawberry preserves instead of salsa. It is yummy! If you opt for the cheese, this recipe would be one to eat the first morning out on an extended trip. Baby Bell mini cheese wheels in a wax casing might be able to keep a little longer.

Yield: Serves 2

Peanut Butter & Banana Wraps

1 tortilla
1 tube/package squeeze peanut butter per tortilla
1 small banana
(Optional) A packet of honey or hazelnut chocolate spread

Slather on the peanut butter and condiments, then cut or lay the banana on the tortilla. Roll and eat.

Note: This one is simple, easy and a snack for some and a meal for others. My son loves these wraps more than anything else for breakfast in the backcountry. You can also borrow the frying pan from another camper who is not "in the know" and heat up the wrap and drizzle the honey or smear the hazelnut chocolate spread over the top when it is warm.

Yield: Serves 1

Morning Potatoes

In a quart freezer bag put:

1/2 cup instant potatoes
1 Tbsp dry milk
Salt and pepper to taste (use single use packets)
2 Tbsp cheese sauce powder
1/2 bag of precooked crumbled bacon.
(Optional) A handful of wasabi peas

In camp: Add 1/2 cup boiling water (sometimes a bit more) and mix well. Fold in wasabi peas just as the mix begins to thicken. Place in cozy and let sit for 5-10 minutes before eating.

Yield: Serves 1

Drinks

Many times while outdoors, I want something to drink with more taste. While I do hear the call of my first aid instructor telling me to drink something with electrolytes, I get tired of sports drinks and the like. This section contains drinks that do taste good, but are not always good for you.

Some of the drinks in this chapter are to be mixed at home in larger amounts and then distributed into multiple small zip top bags, like snack baggies. When in the outdoors you dumb the contents of the baggie into a cup, add the liquid and enjoy.

Tip: In recipes calling for dry milk, you can substitute soy milk powder if you like.

Tip: Try to take double the drink servings you think you might like to have. They are lightweight and I have found I usually want more after drinking the first serving. Also, that person in your group looking with longing eyes at your warm drink will be happy to have it when you toss them a snack bag with drink mix.

Trail Shake

Put in a sandwich bag:

1/3 cup dry milk or powered soy milk
2 Tbsp non-dairy creamer
1 Tbsp custard mix (find in the pudding aisle)
1 envelope breakfast type drink mix (any flavor)

In camp: Put the ingredients into a lexan bottle, add 1 and 1/4 cups cold water and shake very well.

Yield: Serves 1

Night Time Winter Toddy

3-4 Tbsp gelatin mix, flavor of your choice

Mix in a cup with 10 oz hot water. This recipe is excellent for winter camping, especially just before bedtime. Avoid the temptation to use a Lexan bottle, as the Jell-O can gum up the threads.

Yield: Serves 1

Orange Delight Drink

In a snack bag put:

1 tsp orange-flavored instant drink mix
1 tsp dry milk
2 tsp instant vanilla pudding

Dump all the ingredients into a 16 oz mug, add cold water, and stir.

Yield: Serves 1

Spicy Trail Coffee

1 cup instant coffee
1 cup powdered non-dairy creamer
3/4 cup brown sugar
1 1/2 tsp pumpkin pie spice

At home: Combine ingredients in a large bowl. Mix well. Store in an airtight container at home and put individual servings into snack bags to take with you.

At camp: Use 2 tsp of mix per 6 oz of water.

Cappuccino Mix

2/3 cup instant coffee
1 cup powdered non-dairy creamer
1 cup powdered chocolate drink mix
1/2 cup white sugar
3/4 tsp ground cinnamon
1/4 tsp ground nutmeg

At home: Combine ingredients in a large bowl. Mix well. Store in an airtight container at home and put individual servings into snack bags to take with you.

For each 6 oz serving use 3 Tbsp mix.

Yield: Approximately 12 servings

Toasty Eggnog Drink

At home mix together:

1 1/2 cups dry milk
1/2 cup nondairy creamer
1/2 cup powdered egg mix (look in the baking aisle)
2 Tbsp brown sugar
1/2 tsp ground cinnamon
1/2 tsp ground nutmeg

For each 6-8 oz serving use 1/3 cup mix, with cold or hot water.

Winter Coffee

2 cups powdered non-dairy creamer
1 1/2 cups instant hot chocolate mix
1 1/2 cups instant coffee
1 tsp ground cinnamon
1/2 tsp ground nutmeg

At home: Combine ingredients in a large bowl. Mix well. Store in an airtight container at home and put individual servings into snack bags to take with you.

For each 6-8 oz serving use 3 tsp mix. Adjust to taste.

Yield: Approximately 80 servings.

Mocha Au Lait Mix

1 1/2 cups dry milk
1/2 cup instant coffee
1/3 cup brown sugar
2/3 cup miniature semisweet chocolate chips

In a medium bowl, combine milk powder, instant coffee, brown sugar and mini chocolate chips. Mix well. Store in an airtight container at home and put individual servings into snack bags to take with you.

Instructions per serving:
For each 6 oz serving use 1/4 cup mix.

Yield; 12 servings.

Instant Chai Tea Mix I

1 1/2 cups instant tea powder
2 cups powdered non-dairy creamer
1/2 cup dry milk
1 cup confectioner sugar
1/4 cup brown sugar
1 tsp ground ginger
1 tsp ground cinnamon
1 tsp ground cloves
1 tsp ground cardamom
1 tsp ground allspice
1 tsp vanilla powder

Blend well (use a food processor/blender for best results) Store in an airtight container at home and put individual servings into snack bags to take with you.

For each 6-8 oz serving use 1/4 cup mix.

Yield: Approximately 48 servings.

Instant Chai Tea Mix II

1 cup nonfat dry milk
1 cup powdered non-dairy creamer
1 cup French vanilla flavored powdered non-dairy creamer
2 1/2 cups white sugar
1 1/2 cups unsweetened instant tea
2 tsp ground ginger
2 tsp ground cinnamon
1 tsp ground cloves
1 tsp ground cardamom

In a large bowl, combine ingredients. In a blender or food processor, blend 1 cup at a time, until mixture is the consistency of fine powder. Store in an airtight container at home and put individual servings into snack bags to take with you. For each 6-8 oz serving use 2 heaping Tbsp of mix.

Yield: Approximately 36 servings.

Mexican Mocha

At home mix together:

1 1/2 cups instant cocoa mix
1 1/2 cups dry milk
1/2 cup instant coffee
1 tsp ground cinnamon
1 Tbsp dried powdered orange peel

For each 8 oz serving use 1/3 cup mix.

Approximately 10 servings.

Cinnamon Coffee

In a snack sized zip bag put:

1 tsp instant coffee
1/8 tsp cinnamon

Also pack:

1 packet honey.

In camp: Put the mix and honey in your cup and stir well. Add 1 cup boiling water. Stir well and serve.

Yield: Serves 1

Trail Mochas

At home mix:

1 cup instant coffee
1 cup powdered creamer
1/2 cup sugar
1 packet hot cocoa mix (single serving)
3/4 tsp cinnamon

For each 8 oz serving use 2 Tbsp mix. Stir well.

About 20 servings.

Hot Ginger Coconut Smoothie *Lower Sodium*

In a zip snack bag put:

1/4 cup powdered milk
1 Tbsp coconut cream powder
1 Tbsp + 1 tsp sugar
1/2 tsp ground ginger

In camp: Add mix and 1 cup boiling water in a lexan bottle. Shake!

Yield: 1 serving

Toasted Almond Smoothie

At home, blend following until smooth & store in a zip snack bag:

1/2 cup powdered milk
1/4 cup almond paste (can be purchased or made at home)
1 Tbsp sugar
1 Tbsp coconut cream powder

In camp: Add mix, 1 oz amaretto (optional) and 1/2 cup hot water in a lexan bottle. Shake well!

Yield: 1 serving

Salads & Vegetables

One of the things I hated when I first started backpacking was trying to come up with menus and things to eat. After a couple of years I realized that all my meals consisted of just protein and carbohydrates. Rarely did I include vegetables, fruit or anything crunchy that added texture to my meal. This is fine for overnight trips, but for extended trips where variety is a good thing, I craved something else. I learned my lesson on the Wonderland Trail around Mt Rainier in 2004. After a couple days all I could think of was a huge salad or a platter of steamed vegetables. I wanted food with color and crunch.

If this sounds like you, I recommend packing with you a bag of crunchy peas, an apple (if cut up ahead of time, dip in lemon juice), a bag of carrot sticks, carry an orange for breakfast, etc. Fruit and vegetables will last for a couple days if treated carefully. Yes, fresh fruit weighs a little more, but these can hit the spot 2 days in like no other food can, live a little. Freeze-dried and dehydrated items are a great choice for long trips. Add 2 tablespoons to 1/4 cup of dried vegetables per person will give you color, taste and texture. One trick I like is to add wasabi coated dried or freeze-dried peas to a dish. They add a great zing to any recipe and make a good crunchy snack food to eat by the handful too.

Carrot Slaw Trail Salad

In a quart bag put:

2 cups dried shredded cabbage
1 cup dried carrots (from Just Veggies or home dried)
1/2 cup dried pineapple bits and raisins

In a separate container carry (if you have packets, kudos to you):

1 Tbsp sugar
1 Tbsp vinegar
1 Tbsp oil
Salt to taste

In camp: Add cold water to cover the veggies. Let sit for 30 minutes or so. Drain off the liquid, and add the dressing. Toss well.

Yield: Serves 4-6 as a side dish.

Carrot/Pineapple Crunch

1 large lemon peel, grated
1 cup sugar
1/2 cup lemon juice
4 large carrots, peeled and shredded
1 8 oz can crushed pineapple, drained
1 tablespoon toasted slivered almonds

At home: In a saucepan, stir the lemon zest and sugar into the lemon juice in and simmer gently until the sugar is dissolved. Put the carrots and pineapple in a bowl, pour the juice mixture over them, cover the bowl, and marinate for at least 24 hours before drying. Dehydrate until done on vegetable setting.

Package the dried mix in sandwich bags - 1/3 cup of dried salad will make side dishes for two people. Package the almonds separately.

In camp: Add an equal amount of water to each portion of salad (1/3 cup of water to 1/3 cup of salad) and allow to reconstitute for at least half an hour. Add almonds and serve.

Yield: 1 cup (6 side dishes).

Veggie & Bacon Salad

In a quart bag put:

1 cup freeze-dried veggies (peas work well, or use an assortment)

Also take:

2 Tbsp parmesan cheese (4 packets worth)
2 fast food containers of ranch dressing (or about 3 oz worth)
1 bag (2 1/2 - 3 oz) of shelf-stable precooked bacon (You will only use half the bag, so save the rest for another meal the next day)

In camp: Add 1 cup cold water to the vegetables. Let sit for 10 minutes, laying the bag on its side to aid rehydration. Drain off any extra water. Toss in the parmesan and bacon. Stir. Add dressing, mix and enjoy.

Yield: Serves 1 as lunch, 2 as a side dish.

Note: This is a salad that salad haters will love.

Mexi-Bean Salad

1 Tbsp minced cilantro
1/2 tsp salt
1 Tbsp vinegar
1/3 cup salsa
1 15 oz can kidney beans, rinsed and drained
1 cup frozen corn, thawed
1/2 bell pepper, sliced into strips
2 scallions, chopped

At home: Stir the cilantro, salt, and vinegar into the salsa in a large bowl. Add the remaining ingredients, stir, cover the bowl, and marinate for at least 24 hours before drying. The salad is done when the beans are crunchy and the corn is still a bit leathery. Place a single serving - 1/4 cup of the dried mix in each sandwich bag.

In camp: Add an equal amount of water to each portion of salad (1/4 cup of water to 1/4 cup of salad) and allow it to reconstitute for at least 1 hour. Use as a side salad or as filling for a veggie burrito - just add cheese and rice.

Yield: 1 1/2 to 2 cups (6 to 8 side dishes)

Oriental Cabbage Salad

1/4 cup vinegar
1 cup sugar
1/2 tsp salt
1/2 cup vegetable oil
1/4 cup soy sauce
1 large Chinese cabbage, shredded
1 bunch scallions, chopped, white bulb discarded
1 tsp toasted sesame seeds
1 Tbsp toasted slivered almonds

At home: Mix the vinegar, sugar, salt, oil, and soy sauce in a bowl and stir until the sugar is dissolved. Place the cabbage and scallions in a bowl, pour the marinade over them, and toss to thoroughly coat the vegetables. Marinate for 24 to 36 hours, and then dehydrate until dry. Package a single serving - 1/4 cup of the dried mix in a sandwich bag. Pack the sesame seeds and almonds in a separate bag.

In camp: Add 1/8-1/4 cup of water to dried mix and let it soak for at least half an hour. Sprinkle with the sesame seeds and almonds just before serving.

Yield: 1 1/2 to 2 cups (6 to 8 side dishes).

Zucchini Apple Salad

1/4 cup lemon juice
1 Tbsp minced fresh ginger
2 Tbsp sugar
1 large zucchini, shredded
1 large apple, cored and shredded

At home: Combine the lemon juice, ginger, and sugar in a bowl and stir until the sugar dissolves. Place the zucchini and apple in another bowl, pour the juice mixture over them, cover, and marinate for at least 24 hours before dehydrating.

Package a single serving - 1/3 cup of the dried salad in a sandwich bag.

In camp: Add 1/3 cup of water to 1/3 cup of salad and allow it to reconstitute for at least half an hour.

Yield: 1 to 1 1/3 cups (4 side dishes).

Tabbouleh Salad

In a sandwich bag put:

1/2 cup bulgur wheat
4 Tbsp dried parsley
2 Tbsp dried leeks
4 sun dried tomato slices, diced
1/8 tsp salt (a pinch)
1 tsp dried mint

Carry with you 2 tsp lemon juice (or 2 packets) and 1 Tbsp olive oil (1 packet).

In camp: add 1 cup cold water to your bag, and let soak for 30 minutes. Drain, then add the lemon juice and olive oil. Mix well.

Yield: Serves 2-3.

Cole Slaw

In a sandwich bag put:

1 cup dried thinly shredded cabbage
1 Tbsp dried chives

Also take with you:

2 packets sugar or sweetener
1 packet salt

Carry in a leak proof container:
1 1/2 tsp white vinegar (1 packet)
1 1/2 tsp oil (1 packet)

In camp: Soak the cabbage in cold water for 20-30 minutes. Drain the cabbage squeezing the bag well to get out the water. Shake the sugar and salt with the liquids, then toss with the cabbage.

Yield: Serves 4-6, this makes quite a bit.

Carrot Raisin Salad

In a sandwich bag put:

1/2 cup dried grated carrots (if using freeze-dried, soak for about half the time)
1/4 cup golden raisins

Also take:

1 packet sugar or sweetener
1/4 tsp salt (take a small packet)

Carry in a leak proof container:

1 tsp vinegar (1 packet)
1 tsp oil (1 packet)

In camp: Soak the carrots and raisins in enough cold water to cover, for 20-30 minutes. Add the dry ingredients to the liquids and shake well. Toss with the carrot mixture.

Yield: Serves 3

Simple Trail Salad

1 ready-to-eat "complete" bagged salad – get one with dressing, cheese, toppings.
Cherry tomatoes (2 - 4 per person)
1 sandwich bag per person

In camp: Cut the bag open, toss in the dressing and toppings. Roll the bag down or pinch shut and shake well. Serve in bags and top with tomatoes.

Yield: Serves 2-8.

Note: In cooler weather this is one of my favorite things to pack in. It is simple and easy to grab on the way out of town. I have gotten used to eating salad with a spoon, but with a few moments of time one can whittle chopsticks on the trail.

Vegetables

Cabbage & Apples

In a quart freezer bag put:

1/2 cup dried shredded cabbage
3 diced apple rings

Also take:

1 packet sugar
1 Tbsp lemon juice or a couple packets

In camp: Add 1 cup boiling water and let sit for 10 minutes. Drain and add sugar and lemon juice. Shake well. This can be eaten warm or chilled in a creek.

Yield: Serves 2

Curried Corn

In a quart freezer bag put:

1 cup freeze-dried corn

Also take in a small bag:

1 tsp butter powder
1/4 tsp curry powder

In camp: Add 1 cup near boiling water. Let sit in a cozy for 10 minutes. Drain and add seasonings. Stir well.

Yield: Serves 2

Oriental Green Beans

In a quart freezer bag put;

1 cup freeze-dried green beans

Also take:

1-2 Tbsp seasoned rice vinegar
1 Tbsp sesame seeds

In camp: Add 1 cup near boiling water to the beans. Let sit in a cozy for 10 minutes. Drain, splash on vinegar and toss with sesame seeds.

Yield: Serves 2

Buttery Trail Carrots

In a quart freezer bag put:

1/2 cup diced dried carrots

Also take in a small bag:

1 tsp butter powder
1 Tbsp sesame seeds

In camp: Add 1 cup near boiling water, put in a cozy for 10 minutes. Drain, toss with seasonings.

Yield: Serves 2

Soups

Soup and stew to me is a staple of life that is overlooked quite often in the backcountry. When I do see them being consumed it is usually some bland, over salted package that is water, a few veggies and some noodles. Soup and stew are what winter is all about to me. There is nothing like sipping on a warm helping of chowder while sitting in a winter wonderland. They are an excellent choice when you are too tired to make a full dinner. They warm you, rehydrate you and for some reason make you feel good on an emotional level. Match it up with some bread or a bagel and cheese you carried in. When it is cold outside, I know this is all I need sometimes.

I like to eat some soups out of a mug, you can do it in a freezer bag if you use something like a Fozzil® or Orikaso® brand bowl.

While some of the recipes in the section do call for dried soup mixes, some do not and if you start researching you can find lower sodium equivalents or make your own soup bases pretty darn easy. The FBC web site has a lot more healthy soup ideas on it as well.

Clam Chowder

In a quart freezer bag put:

1 cup instant mashed potatoes
1/2 cup dried milk
1/2 tsp dill
1/2 tsp black pepper
1/2 tsp thyme
1/2 tsp granulated garlic
1/2 tsp salt

Also take:

3 oz. pouch of clams
2 packets parmesan cheese

In camp: Put the clams in the freezer bag, and add 2 cups boiling water. Stir well, pop in a cozy and let sit for 10 minutes. Top with parmesan.

Yields: Serves 1 or 2 as a starter course.

Potato Soup

In a quart freezer bag put:

1 Tbsp dry onion
1 package dried potatoes (flavor of your choice, 2 cup water package)
1 Tbsp dried bell peppers

Also take:
1 small bag shelf stable crumbled bacon (2 1/2 - 3 oz)
Packets of salt and pepper.

Add 3 cups boiling water and bacon, stir well. Put in a cozy for 10 minutes. Season to taste.

Yield: Serves 2 or 3 as a starter course.

Bean & Potato Chowder

In a quart freezer bag put:

1 1/2 tsp low sodium bouillon
1/3 cup dry milk
1/4 cup instant refried beans
2/3 cup instant potatoes
2 Tbsp shelf stable parmesan cheese
1 tsp butter powder
Pinch of granulated garlic

In camp: Add 1 1/2 to 1 3/4 cups boiling water. Stir well and let sit for 5 minutes.

Yield: Serves 1 or 2 as a starter course.

Salmon Chowder

Put in a quart freezer bag:

1/2 cup instant mashed potatoes
1/2 cup dry milk
1 tsp Old Bay® seasoning
1 tsp dried chives
2 Tbsp freeze-dried veggies
1/2 tsp granulated garlic
1/2 tsp salt

Also take:

3 oz. pouch of salmon
2-4 packets parmesan cheese

In camp: Put the salmon in the freezer bag, and add 2 cups boiling water. Stir well, put in a cozy for 10 minutes. Top with parmesan cheese.

Yield: Serves 1 or 2 as a starter course.

Note: On Halloween 2004, I sat in the snow below Bandera Mountain with my friend Tori. My lunch that clear cold day was Salmon Chowder. That was the day we came up with the original idea of having a FBC website.

Seafood Chowder

Put in a quart freezer bag:

1/2 cup instant mashed potatoes
1/2 cup dry milk
1 Tbsp butter powder
1 tsp Old Bay® seasoning
A couple shakes of celery seed

Also take 1 3 oz. pouch each of shrimp and crab meat (can substitute clams)

In camp: Add the seafood, and 2 cups boiling water. Stir well, and put in a cozy for 5-10 minutes.

Yields: Serves 1 or 2 as a starter course.

Lucky's Hearty Clam Chowder

Put in a quart freezer bag:

1 package leek soup mix
1 cup instant mashed potatoes

Also take with you 1 3 oz. pouch of clams or a can of baby clams in oil.

In camp: Add 2 cups boiling water to the freezer bag; add the clams and the margarine. Stir well and serve.

Put in a cozy for 5 minutes. Season to taste with salt & pepper.

Yields: Serves 1 or 2 as a starter course.

Bacon & Potato Chowder

In a quart freezer bag put:

1 Tbsp dried onion flakes
3 Tbsp shelf stable bacon pieces
1 Tbsp dried carrots
1/2 cup instant hash browns (they come in a paper "milk box" container)
1 envelope creamy chicken soup mix (1 cup size)
1/3 cup dry milk

In camp: Add 2 cups boiling water, stir and add the bacon in. Put in cozy for 10 minutes. Stir well again.

Yield: Serves 1 or 2 as a starter course.

Sushi Bowl *Vegetarian*

In a quart freezer bag put:

1 cup instant white rice
1/2 cup dried veggies
1-2 sheets nori seaweed, cut into 1 inch squares
1/2 tsp sugar

Also take:

1-2 packets soy sauce

In camp: Add 1 1/4 boiling water, put in a cozy for 10 minutes. Add 1-2 packets soy sauce to taste.

Yield: Serves 1

Curried Rice Soup

In a quart freezer bag put:

1 package green pea soup (Lipton Cup of Soup® on both items, single serving)
1 package tomato soup
1/3 cup dry milk
1/2 - 1 tsp curry powder
1/2 cup instant rice

Also take 1-2 packets parmesan cheese

In camp: Add 2 cups boiling water, stir well. Put in a cozy for 10 minutes and eat. Top with parmesan cheese and serve.

Yield: Serves 1 or 2 as a starter course.

Noodle Soup

In a quart freezer bag put:

1/4 cup crushed ramen noodles
1 tsp low sodium bouillon
1/4 cup freeze-dried vegetables
1/4 tsp granulated garlic

1 package of chicken (optional)

In camp: Add 1 cup boiling water, put in a cozy for 10 minutes. Stir again and serve.

Yield: Serves 1

Minestrone Soup

In a quart freezer bag put:

2 tsps chicken bouillon
1/2 cup instant refried bean flakes (use brown or black)
1/4 cup freeze-dried vegetables
1/4 cup couscous
1/4 tsp granulated garlic
1/2 tsp dried parsley
1/4 tsp salt

Tape to freezer bag, 2 salt packets and 1 pepper packet.

In camp: Add 2 cups boiling water, stir well, seal and put in cozy for 10-15 minutes. This soup is almost chowder thickness, so if you like it thinner, add 3 cups water instead of the original 2, but add 1 tsp extra bouillon.

Yield: Serves 1 or 2 as a starter course.

Note: I came up with this recipe while on a snowshoeing daytrip at Hurricane Ridge in the Olympic Mountains. We sat in the snow sipping the soup and munching on bagels from the best bagel shop in Washington State, the Olympic Bagel Co. in Port Angeles.

Rainrunner's Cheesy Chicken Rice Soup

In a quart freezer bag put:

1/2 cup instant rice
3 Tbsp cheese sauce powder
1 Tbsp dry milk
1 Tbsp freeze-dried vegetables
1/4 tsp salt or to taste

Also take along a 5 oz can of chicken.

In camp: Add 1 cup boiling water and chicken with liquid. Stir, put in a cozy and let sit for 5-10 minutes.

Yield: Serves 1

Lunch

The hardest meal for most trips seems to always be lunch. It is pushed to the back of planning. Usually lunchtime is not when one wants to stop, unload half of your gear to get to a stove or spend an hour doing prep and cleanup. So you see too many people eating protein bars, energy goo, bags of trail mix, summer sausage or candy bars for "lunch". You will be thankful when your friends are eating protein bars and you have a nice lunch that actually tastes great, smells good and keeps you going all afternoon. Talk about a conversation piece at lunch! I cannot count the number of times a new person in my hiking group has a perplexed look on their face as they see what the rest of us have and then look down at their so called "lunch". It always reminds me of elementary school, sitting at the lunch table and that one kid who had nothing more than a smooshed peanut butter and jelly sandwich with nothing to trade.

For the recipes in this section that can take any temperature water if it calls for it, add the water to the bag twenty minutes or so minutes before you think you might want lunch. Otherwise your compatriots may be packing up to leave your appointed lunch spot just as you are getting ready to eat. For example, you are feeling a little hungry and think you or the group will stop in about a half an hour or so. Take the freezer bag out containing your meal, put the proper amount of water in the bag, mix everything up, push the air out, then set the bag back in your pack, bag, pouch or wherever you can put it. Just remember to think ahead. It will be worth it.

Ramen Salad

Put in a freezer bag:

1 package of ramen noodles (just the noodles!)
2 Tbsp freeze-dried mixed vegetables

Take 1 packet salad dressing of choice (shelf stable, or use 2 tubs of Ranch dip)

Add 1 1/2 cups water (any temperature), squeeze the air out and seal the bag. Let sit for 30 minutes to 1 hour. Drain well. Add dressing and toss well. This is really good with cubed cheese, pepperoni slices or whatever you feel like adding.

Yield: Serves 1

Spinach Couscous

At home in a bowl mix:

1 cup couscous
1 pkg cream of spinach or broccoli soup mix pouch
3 Tbsp milk or soy milk powder
1 pouch (3 oz) of tuna, salmon or chicken per freezer bag.

At home: Mix all ingredients into a bowl and separate equally into two quart freezer bags. Each bag gets a pouch of meat with it.

When ready to eat, add approximately 1 cup of water and stir well. Let sit for 20-30 minutes or so, add meat and enjoy.

Yield: Serves 1 per bag.

Tomato Couscous Salad

In a quart freezer bag put:

1/4 cup couscous
3 Tbsp finely chopped toasted almonds
1/4 tsp dried basil
1/8 tsp granulated garlic
2 Tbsp finely diced sun dried tomatoes

When ready, add 1/2 cup water. Stir well and let sit for 15-20 minutes.

Yield: Serves 1

Note: If you would like a hot salad, boil the water and set it aside for 10 minutes.

Tortilla Roll-Ups/Wraps

Chicken Tomato Wraps

In a quart freezer bag put:

2 Tbsp dried tomato bits/flakes
1 Tbsp parmesan cheese
1 Tsp dried onion
1 tsp dried bell pepper flakes
1/2 tsp Italian herbs
1/4 tsp granulated garlic
Salt to taste

Also take one 7 oz pouch of chicken and 2 tortillas.

When ready, add 3 Tbsp near boiling water to the bag. Let sit for 10 minutes, stir and add the chicken. Mix well and serve on the tortillas.

Yield: Serves 1-2 depending on how hungry you are.

Cheese Herb Wraps

In a sandwich bag put:

1/4 cup cheese sauce powder
3/4 tsp granulated garlic
3/4 tsp Italian herb blend
1 tortilla or bag of chips

When ready, add 1 Tbsp water, start mixing and add 1 Tbsp of water at a time as needed. Spread on tortillas, dip chips, etc.

Chicken Rolls

1 foil pouch chicken
1-3 packets of mayo or ranch dip tubs
1 packet of relish, salsa or flavor you like.
4 soft taco sized tortillas or flatbreads.

Mix in pouch, spread on tortillas. Also great with cheddar or Swiss cheese added.

Yield: Serves 1-2

Note: This is one of my favorite lunches. If you are eating it first day out, bring a bag of shredded lettuce to put with it.

Hummus Wraps

In a quart bag put:

1/4 cup hummus mix
2 tortillas or flatbreads per person
(Optional) 1/2 tsp curry or other spices
(Optional) 3 oz of chicken

When ready, add 1/4 cup cold water and mix well. A packet of lemon juice is nice to add to the hummus. Spread on tortilla or flatbread.

Yield: Serves 1
Note: For first day out add cucumber slices and cheese. A packet or tub of ranch dressing goes well here too.

Trail Chicken Salad

1 - 7 oz pouch of chicken
2-4 packets mayonnaise
1-2 tsp curry in a small zip bag.
2-4 soft taco tortillas or flatbreads.

Squeeze the mayo into the chicken bag, then shake the curry on top, mix it in a bit, then mix into the chicken.

Yield: Serves 2

Note: If you are having this first day out, carry 1/2 cup of diced bell peppers to toss in. This is one of my favorite lunches.

Tuna Salad Wraps

1 foil pouch of tuna (3 oz.)
1 packet mayo
1 packet relish
2 soft taco tortillas

Open tuna pouch, add mayo and relish, mix up, and put on tortillas.

Yield: Serves 1

Note: If eating your first day out, carrying in shredded lettuce, diced carrots or bell peppers adds a lot of crunch and good texture.

Peanut Butter Wraps

Tortillas or flat bread
1 Jiffy squeeze tube of peanut butter per tortilla
1 packet honey or Nutella®
Snack boxes of raisins

Spread and enjoy.

Note: Simple, easy, packs very well. My son loves these on the trail. If you use a bear canister or Ursack®, soft taco size tortillas will fit on the bottom perfectly.

Dinner

When I am in the backcountry, my strongest menu planning is dinner time. My tent is set up, my sleeping bag is fluffed, I am tired from a good long hike and ready for something warm in my stomach. For me there is nothing like a hot meal after a long day in the outdoors. I want food that is easy to prepare, but smells and tastes so good I'll eat it up. While many will say if you are hungry enough you will eat almost anything, why even put yourself in that situation? Bring something you know you will like and will fill you up.

As a side note, backpacking with my son made my food preparation a bit more interesting. I have to find meals that he will eat and keep him going. This is a special challenge. Some of the recipes in the section take this into account. While there is a book in the Freezer Bag Cooking™ series that is currently in development and specifically targeted at kids and scouts, in the mean time, recipes here should serve you and your kids well.

Rice based meals:

Basic rice cooking:

Serving sizes:

1 person: 1 cup rice/1 cup water
2 persons: 2 cups rice/ 2 cups water

You can find white, premium white, brown and wild rice. Sometimes, instant rice needs a pinch of salt and flavorings added. Rice can handle sweet or savory flavors well. After you add your boiling water, stir and put your rice in a cozy for 5-10 minutes.

Cranberry Chicken Rice

In a quart freezer bag put:

1 cup instant rice
1 tsp low sodium chicken bullion
1/4 tsp salt
1/2 tsp granulated garlic
1 tsp parsley
1 tsp. dried onions
2 Tbsp freeze-dried vegetables
3 Tbsp dried cranberries

Also take a 5 oz. can of chicken

In camp: Put the chicken (with liquid) into the freezer bag, and 1 1/4 cups boiling water. Stir well, seal and put in a cozy for 10 minutes.

Yield: Serves 1

Note: In fall of 2004 I ate this along the banks of the Skokomish River in Olympic NP. It was a meal that changed a lot of my hiking partner's views on FBC cooking. It is one of my favorite recipes to make. It is simple, it smells so good and it warms you up inside. For an added bonus, substitute a 1/4 cup instant wild rice for the white rice.

Four Cheese Hamburger Rice

In a quart freezer bag put:

1 cup instant rice
1/3 cup instant milk
1 package Four Cheese sauce blend (in pasta aisle)
1/2 tsp butter powder
1/2 cup dehydrated hamburger

In camp: Add 1 1/2 cups boiling water, stir well and put in a cozy for 10 minutes. Stir and eat.

Yield: Serves 1

Note: A bit salty, but it feels like you are eating a white trash casserole on the trail. Kids love it.

Creamy Spinach Rice & Hamburger

In a quart freezer bag put:

2 cups instant rice
1 pkg cream of spinach soup mix
1/2 cup dried hamburger

Also take 4 packets parmesan cheese

In camp: Add 2 1/2 cups boiling water to the bag, and stir very well. Seal and let sit in a cozy for 10 minutes. Stir again, top with the parmesan cheese and serve.

Yield: Serves 2

Note: My son loves this recipe. I made it for him on a backpacking trip at Mt. Rainier NP and he ate 2/3 rd of the bag! It feels like you are having a comfort casserole.

Veggie Hamburger Rice

In a quart freezer bag put:

2 cups instant rice
1 pkg Knorr® Spring Vegetable Soup Mix
1/2 cup dried hamburger

In camp: Add 2 1/4 cups boiling water, stir well and put in a cozy for 10 minutes. Stir again and serve. Add cheese on top if desired.

Yield: Serves 2

Note: This is another kid friendly meal. My son eats it without noticing it has vegetables in it.

Wild & White Creamy Rice

In a quart freezer bag put:

1 1/2 cups instant white rice
1/4 cup instant wild rice
1/4 cup freeze-dried veggies
1 pkg cream of spinach soup mix
1/3 cup dry milk

Also take one 5 oz can of chicken.

In camp: Dump the can of chicken with liquid into the bag. Add 2 cups boiling water and stir well. Put in a cozy and let sit 10 minutes. Stir again and serve.

Yield: Serves 2

Creamy Carbonara Rice

In a quart freezer bag put:

2 cups instant rice
1 package carbonara sauce packet (in the pasta aisle)
1/2 cup dry milk
1/4 cup freeze-dried vegetables

Also take a 5 oz can of chicken

In camp: Add 2 1/2 cups near boiling water and chicken with liquid to bag. Stir very well, put in cozy for 10 minutes. Stir again and serve.

Yield: Serves 2

Creamy Spinach Veggie Rice

In a quart freezer bag put:

1 pkg Knorr® Cream of Spinach soup mix
1/3 cup dry milk
1 1/2 cups instant rice
1/4 cup freeze-dried vegetables

Also bring a 5 oz can of chicken.

In camp: Dump the chicken with liquid in the bag, and 1 3/4 cups near boiling water. Stir well, put in a cozy for 10 minutes. Stir well.

Yield: Serves 2

Cheesy Chicken Veggie Rice

In a quart freezer bag put:

1 cup instant rice
1/4 cup freeze-dried vegetables
2 Tbsp cheese sauce powder
2 Tbsp dry milk
Pinch of salt

Also take a 5 oz can of chicken.

In camp: Dump the chicken with liquid into the bag. Add 1 1/4 cups near boiling water, mix well and put in cozy for 5-10 minutes. Stir, and let set for another minute to thicken.

Yield: Serves 1

Note: Picky children will usually eat this meal with a smile. It is a good way to get protein and veggies into them. If you leave the veggies out, subtract a 1/4 cup of water.

Cheesy White & Wild Chicken Rice

In a quart freezer bag put:

1 1/2 cups instant rice
1/4 cup instant wild rice
3 Tbsp cheese sauce powder
2 Tbsp dry milk
2 Tbsp parmesan cheese
1 Tbsp dried onion
Pinch of granulated garlic

Also take a 5 oz can of chicken.

In camp: Dump the chicken with liquid in the bag, and add 1 3/4 cups near boiling water. Stir well, and put in a cozy for 10 minutes. Stir again and serve.

Yield: Serves 2

Curry Cashew Rice

In a quart freezer bag put:

2 cups instant rice
1/2 cup dry milk
3 tsp curry powder
1 tsp salt

Also bring:

1/2 cup chopped cashew pieces (in a zip snack bag)
3 oz of cheese (grated)
1 pouch chicken (7 oz)

In camp: Add chicken, 2 cups of near boiling water, stir well and put in a cozy for 10 minutes. When ready, sprinkle cheese in bag, add nuts and serve.

Yield: Serves 2

Curried Thai Chicken Rice

In a quart freezer bag put:

3/4 cup instant white rice
1/8 cup instant brown rice
1/8 cup instant wild rice
1 Tbsp curry powder
1 Tbsp coconut cream powder
1 tsp low sodium bouillon

Also take:

1/2 to 1 Tbsp chunky peanut butter (1 packet)
1 pouch chicken (7 oz)

In camp: Add the peanut butter, chicken and 1 cup near boiling water. Stir well and put in a cozy for 10 minutes.

Yield: Serves 1-2

Chicken Almond Rice

In a quart freezer bag put:

2 cups instant rice
2 Tbsp dried onion
1 tsp low sodium chicken bouillon
1/3 cup golden raisins

Also take:

1 pouch chicken (7 oz)
1 small package sliced almonds

In camp: Add chicken and 2 cups near boiling water, stir very well, put in cozy for 10 minutes.

Yield: Serves 2

Creamy Almond Chicken Rice

In a quart freezer bag put:

2 cups instant rice
1 Tbsp dried onion
2 packets cream of chicken soup (1 cup size)
3 oz slivered almonds

Also take 1 5 oz can of chicken

In camp: Add the chicken (liquid and all) and 2 cups near boiling water. Stir well, and put in a cozy for 10 minutes.

Yield: Serves 2

Curried Vegetable Chicken

In a quart freezer bag put:

2 cups instant rice
1 package Knorr® Vegetable soup mix
3 Tbsp dry milk
1/4 cup freeze-dried vegetable mix
1 Tbsp curry powder

Also take:

1 5 oz can of chicken

In two separate snack bags put:

2 oz shredded coconut
2 oz golden raisins

In camp: Add chicken (liquid and all) and 2 1/2 cups near boiling water to the bag. Stir and put in a cozy for 10-15 minutes. Add coconut and raisins to taste.

Yield: Serves 2

Creamy Brown Rice Chicken

In a quart freezer bag put:

1 cup instant brown rice
1/4 cup slivered almonds
1/4 cup freeze-dried mushrooms
2 Tbsp dried onion
1 Tbsp dried green or red bell peppers
1 packet cream of chicken soup (1 cup size)

Also take 1 5 oz can of chicken

In camp: Add chicken (liquid and all) and 1 1/2 cups near boiling water. Stir well and let sit in a cozy for 15 minutes.

Yield: Serves 1

Veggie Brown Rice *Low Sodium*

In a quart freezer bag put:

1 cup instant brown rice
1/2 cup freeze-dried vegetable mix
1 tsp low sodium bouillon-flavor of your choice
Pinch of salt
1/4 tsp dried thyme & parsley

In camp: Add 1 1/2 cups near boiling water to bag. Stir well and let sit for 15 minutes in a cozy.

Yield: Serves 1

Note: This recipe also works well as a wrap filling with slices of swiss cheese added.

Creamy Chicken for Very Hungry Hikers

In a quart freezer bag put:

1 cup instant brown rice
2 packets cream of chicken soup (1 cup size)
1/4 cup slivered almonds
1/4 cup freeze-dried mushrooms
2 Tbsp dry onion
1 Tbsp dried green or red pepper flakes
1/2 tsp salt
(Optional) Add spices to taste

Also take:

2 (7 oz) pouches of chicken (don't drain)

In camp: Dump the chicken into the bag and add 1 1/2 cups near boiling water. Stir well and let sit a cozy for 10 minutes.

Yield: Serves 2

Creamy Spinach Chicken Rice

In a quart freezer bag put:

2 cups instant rice
1 package cream of spinach soup mix
1/4 freeze-dried vegetables

Also take:

1 can of chicken (5 oz)

In camp: Add the chicken with broth and 2 1/4 cups near boiling water, stir well and put in a cozy for 10 minutes.

Yield: Serves 1-2

Chicken, Noodles & Rice

In a quart freezer bag put:

1 package instant chicken noodle soup (1 cup size)
1 cup instant rice
1/4 cup freeze-dried vegetables

Also take:

1 pouch of chicken (7 oz)

In camp: Add the chicken and 2 1/4 cups near boiling water, stir and put in a cozy for 10 minutes.

Yield: Serves 1

Note: If you would like it more like a casserole, use less water.

Bulk Brown Rice & Chicken *Low Sodium*

2 cups freeze-dried chicken
1 cup freeze-dried peas
6 cups instant brown rice
4 Tbsp curry powder
1 Tbsp black pepper
6 tsp low sodium chicken bouillon
1 cup nuts
1 cup raisins

Add together everything but nuts and raisins. Pack 1 cup per person with a handful of nuts and raisins packed in a separate bag.

In camp: Add 1 cup near boiling water, stir well and put in a cozy for 10 minutes. Sprinkle on nuts and raisins.

Yield: About 6 servings. Adjust water to taste.

Vegetarian/Vegan Rice Curry *Low Sodium*

In a quart freezer bag put:

1 cup instant rice
1 Tbsp dry onion
2 tsp curry powder (or to taste)
1 Tbsp coconut cream powder
salt to taste
1/8 cup each of dried apricots, raisins, dates and pears, chopped small.
1/8 cup of cashews, almonds or peanuts, chopped small.

In camp: Add 1 cup of near boiling water, stir well and let sit in a cozy for 5-10 minutes. Stir and enjoy.

Yield: Serves 1

Spicy Pork & Rice

In a quart freezer bag put:

1 cup instant rice
1/2 cup dried pork (found in Asian markets)
1/4 cup freeze-dried peas
1/2 tsp sugar
Salt and pepper to taste

Also take:

1-2 packets of hot sauce
1 packet olive oil

In camp: Add 1 1/4 cups near boiling water, the oil & hot sauce packets. Stir well and put in a cozy for 10 minutes.

Yield: Serves 1

Black Beans, Beef and Rice

In a quart freezer bag put:

1 package black bean soup (think individual cups of soup such as Nile Spice®, etc)
1/4 cup dried ground beef
1/2 cup instant rice
1/2 tsp crushed red pepper
1 Tbsp dry onion

In camp: Add 1 1/2 cups near boiling water to the bag, stir well and put in a cozy for 10 minutes.

Yield: Serves 1

Vegetable Beef Rice *Low Sodium*

In a quart freezer bag put:

1 cup instant rice
1/4 cup freeze-dried mixed veggies
1/4 cup dried ground beef
1 tsp dry onion
1 tsp low sodium beef bouillon
Salt to taste

In camp: Add 1 1/2 cups near boiling water to the bag. Stir well and put in a cozy for 10 minutes.

Yield: Serves 1

Creamy Curry Chicken & Rice

In a quart freezer bag put:

1/4 cup freeze-dried chicken
1/2 cup instant rice
1 packet cream of chicken (1 cup size)
1 1/2 tsp curry powder

In camp: Add 1 cup near boiling water and let sit for 10 minutes in a cozy.

Yield: Serves 1

Chinese Take Out

1 can assorted Chinese vegetables
1 can bean sprouts

At home, drain and dehydrate the vegetables till dry. Bag in a quart freezer bag when cool. Store in the freezer till you leave for your trip.

In a second quart freezer bag put:

1 1/2 cups instant rice

Also take:

4-6 packets soy sauce
1 7 oz pouch of chicken

In camp: Cover the dried vegetables with near boiling water and let sit in a cozy for about 10 minutes. During this time, add 1 1/2 cups boiling water to the rice bag. Put in a cozy for 10 minutes. Put the pouch of chicken under to start warming it, or if you have an extra cup, let it sit in a mug full of hot water (still sealed). Drain off any extra water from the vegetables, add in the pouch of chicken, season with soy sauce to taste, and serve over the rice.

Yield: Serves 2

Herb Chicken & Rice *Lower Sodium*

In a quart freezer bag put:

1-1/3 cups instant rice
2 Tbsp dry onion
1/2 tsp sage
2 tsp low sodium chicken bouillon

Also take:

1 can of chicken (5 oz)

In camp: Add the can of chicken with liquid and 1 1/3 cups near boiling water. Mix well and put in a cozy for 10 minutes.

Yield: Serves 1

Chili & Veggie Rice *Low Sodium and Vegetarian*

In a quart freezer bag put:

1 1/2 cups instant rice
1/2 cup freeze-dried corn
1 Tbsp Textured Vegetable Protein (TVP)
1 tsp chili powder or to taste (take more with you just in case)
1 tsp granulated garlic
Salt to taste

In camp: Add 2 1/4 cups near boiling water, stir well and leave in a cozy for 15 minutes.

Yield: Serves 1

Salmon Rice

In a quart freezer bag put:

1 package cream of broccoli soup mix
2 cups instant rice
1/2 cup freeze-dried vegetables
1/3 cup dry milk

Also take:

1 large pouch salmon

In camp: Add the salmon and 2 1/2 cups near boiling water. Stir well, put in a cozy for 10 minutes.

Yield: Serves 2

Grits & Cheesy Veggies

In a quart freezer bag put:

1 packet instant grits
1/3 cup freeze-dried peas
1/3 cup freeze-dried mushrooms
2 tsp butter powder
2 Tbsp cheese sauce powder

In camp: Add 1 1/2 cups near boiling water, stir well, and put in a cozy for 10 minutes.

Yield: Serves 1

Couscous Dishes

Couscous cooking tips:

You can use couscous in boxes or for a better buy, find it in bulk. Couscous is made from seminola, the same as pasta, it is pasta, it just doesn't need anything but a little water. If you want to cook it, use near boiling water, otherwise you can eat many dishes by just using cold water with couscous. You can find couscous in regular, whole wheat and flavored varieties these days.

Basic cooking method:

1 person: 1/3 cup couscous to 1/2 cup water
2 persons: 3/4 cup couscous to 1 cup water

To this you can add whatever flavorings, herbs or spices you might desire. A pinch of salt is usually mandatory with couscous. I always take salt packets with me to be sure. Couscous works well with either savory or sweet recipes and handles items like nuts and dried fruit well. It does not do well though with heavy thick sauces.

Add your near boiling water, stir well, and put in a cozy for 5-10 minutes.

Cheesy Couscous

In a quart freezer bag put:

1/2 cup couscous
3 Tbsp. cheese sauce powder
1/4 tsp. salt
1 Tbsp dry milk

In camp: Add 1 cup near boiling water, mix well and seal the bag. Let sit for 10 minutes, stir again. Add 3 oz of chicken if you so desire.

Yield: Serves 1

Note: This is one of my son's favorite meals for backpacking. Every mom I know who has served it to their kids agrees it works very well. Think of it as instant mac & cheese!

Salmon Craisin Coucous Pilaf *Lower Sodium*

In a quart freezer bag put:

3/4 cup couscous
1 tsp low sodium bouillon
1 tsp dried parsley
1/4 tsp granulated garlic
1/4 tsp salt
1/4 cup dried cranberries

Also take:

1 pouch of salmon (3 oz)

In camp: Add the salmon pouch and 1 cup near boiling water, stir and put in a cozy for 10 minutes. Fluff and serve.

Yield: Serves 1-2

Curry Couscous

In a quart freezer bag put:

3/4 cup couscous
2 Tbsp. coconut cream powder
2 Tbsp. freeze-dried vegetables
2 tsp. curry powder (If you aren't used to curry you can use less)
1/4-1/2 tsp. salt
1/2 tsp. ginger powder

Also take:

1 pouch of chicken (7 oz)

In camp: Add the chicken and 1 1/4 cups near boiling water, stir well, seal and put in a cozy for 5 minutes. Stir.

Yield: Serves 2

Note: I like adding chopped peanuts and coconut (use snack bags).

Curried Vegetable Couscous

In a quart freezer bag put:

1/2 pkg vegetable soup mix
1/8 cup dried cranberries or golden raisins
1/4 tsp curry powder
2/3 cup couscous

In camp: Add 1 1/2 cups near boiling water and stir well. Let sit in a cozy for 10 minutes.

Yield: Serves 2

Notes: The recipe works well with a pouch of chicken (7 oz) added. If you carry oil with you, add 1 Tbsp of olive oil.

Crunchy Couscous

In a quart freezer bag put:

10 oz plain couscous
2 tsps low sodium chicken bouillon
Pinch of salt
2 Tbsp dried onion
1/2 cup diced dried apricots
2-3 oz of toasted sliced almonds

Also take one 5 oz can of chicken.

In camp: Put the chicken plus liquid into the bag, and add 1 3/4 cups near boiling water. Stir well, and put in a cozy for 5-10 minutes

Yield: Serves 2

Couscous with Mushrooms & Tomatoes

In a quart freezer bag put:

1/2 cup couscous
4 minced sun dried tomatoes
1/4 cup freeze-dried mushrooms
1 tsp low sodium chicken bouillon
1 Tbsp dried onion
1 tsp parsley flakes
black pepper & salt to taste
1-2 packets of parmesan cheese

In camp: Add 1 1/4 cups near boiling water stir and put in a cozy for 5 minutes. Add parmesan cheese.

Yield: Serves 1

Vegetarian/Vegan Spinach Couscous

In a quart freezer bag put:

1/4 cup dried tofu cubes
1/2 cup dried spinach
1/8 cup freeze-dried veggie flakes
2 Tbsp vegetable broth powder or onion soup mix
1/3 cup couscous

Also take:

1 packet of salt
1 packet of pepper

In camp: Add 1 Tbsp olive oil and 1/2 to 2/3 cup near boiling water. Stir and put in a cozy for 5 minutes. Add salt and pepper to taste.

Yield: Serves 1

Veggie & Tuna Couscous Pilaf

In a quart freezer bag put:

3/4 cup couscous
1/4 cup freeze-dried peas
1 tsp low sodium bouillon
Salt and pepper to taste
1 Tbsp cheese mix

Also take:

1 pouch of tuna (3 oz)

In camp: Add the tuna (break up well in the pouch), 1 1/4 cups near boiling water, and stir. Top with finely chopped cheddar cheese. Put in a cozy and let sit for 5 minutes.

Yield: Serves 1-2 hikers

Simple Couscous Pilaf *Lower Sodium*

In a quart freezer bag put:

1/2 cup couscous
1 tsp red pepper flakes
1 tsp low sodium chicken bouillon
1 tsp granulated garlic

Also take:
Parmesan cheese packets

In camp: Add 1 cup near boiling water, stir, and let sit in a cozy for 10 minutes.

Yield: Serves 1

Veggie Exotic Couscous *Low Sodium*

In a quart freezer bag put:

1/4 cup + 2 Tbsp couscous
1 Tbsp dried cranberries
1 Tbsp golden raisins
2 tsp diced dried carrots
2 tsp dried onion
1 1/2 tsp low sodium chicken bouillon
1 1/2 tsp chili powder
1/2 tsp granulated garlic
1/4 tsp brown sugar

Also take:

2 Tbsp diced toasted almonds

In camp: Add 1/2 cup near boiling water, stir well and let sit in a cozy for 10 minutes. Sprinkle with nuts.

Yield: Serves 1

Pasta

While the recipes in this section call for using ramen as the noodles for convenience reasons, but there is a better option. If you have access to a dehydrator and the inclination, the way to go is to cook and dehydrate pasta at home and substitute it for the ramen in the recipes in the section. To substitute pasta, cook it at home, until "al dente", draine, rinse and dry at 135° in a dehydrator (depending on type, 2-6 hours, till good and dry-you are looking for hard and almost brittle. No flexibility at all.) If you want to use dried pasta in recipes of your own making, the rehydration method is equal pasta to water. I would suggest 1/2 cup of pasta per person if you are adding meat. Otherwise, 1 cup of pasta per person should work fine. In camp add the boiling water to your freezer bag (i.e. 1/2 cup pasta to 1/2 cup water). Seal the bag and put in a cozy for a good 10-15 minutes. Be sure to shake the bag once or twice to make sure the water gets mixed in. After it has cooked, drain and add the sauce. Yes, it sounds crazy to put pasta in water just to dehydrate it, but remember that pasta you buy in the store is just dried, not cooked. So with this process, you cook it at home and then just rehydrate it later on. Trust me, it works great and is way better than using ramen.

Also, commercial vinyl pouches of refrigerated pasta sauce work well for the first night out. Heat the pouch in a mug of boiling water while your pasta cooks. Knorr® and other brands of similar pasta sauce packets are great and can be prepared in the freezer bag when you first do the pasta. If the recipe calls for milk, 1/3 cup dry milk or soy milk powder equals 1 cup milk.

A quick note about using ramen and the sodium question.

Many people have said that using ramen is too high in sodium. This may be true if you prepare ramen per the directions on the package it comes in. Many of the recipes in this section that use ramen omit the little "flavor" packets that come with the ramen or reduce the amount used. The flavor packet is what contains much of the sodium content you see on the nutritional label for the ramen. Eliminate the flavor packet and eliminate much of the sodium. So what do you replace the flavor that the packet would normally provide you ask? There are plenty of low sodium spice options in your local grocery store's spice aisle. These can be put in the freezer bag when preparing at home instead of using the ramen flavor packet. Just remember, for most people, the amount of sodium in a packet of ramen, with the flavor packet, is not a big deal.

If you are a person who is sensitive to sodium, check the companion web site for this book (http://www.freezerbagcooking.com/). We keep an up to date list of good low/no sodium spices that we use and have a lot more low/no sodium recipes. FBC is about options, so feel free to spice up the meals.

Ramen made simple, easy & tasty

Cooking directions:

1 block of ramen, per person, per quart freezer bag. 1 1/2 cups boiling water, per bag. Put in a cozy for 5 -10 minutes.

Ramen can also be done with cold water, let sit for 10 minutes and drain.

Additions to ramen:

Protein:

Bagged bacon
Canned chicken
Pouched meats
Freeze dried tofu
First night out-bagged Canadian bacon.

Other items:

Sun dried tomatoes (add with boiling water)
Freeze dried vegetables (add with boiling water)
Butter powder
Parmesan cheese
Cheddar cheese
BBQ sauce
Ranch dressing
Olive oil
Butter
Herbs & spices

Ramen Pad Thai

In a quart freezer bag put:

1 block spicy chicken ramen (depending on taste, 1/4 to all of flavor packet)

Also take:

1 5 oz can chicken breast (drain before using)
1 Tbsp of peanut butter (individual packets work well)

Put 1 1/2 cups boiling water into the ramen. Put in a cozy for 10 minutes.
Drain off most of the liquid. Add and stir in Chicken and peanut butter.

Yield: Serves 1

Parmesan Veggie Noodles

In a quart freezer bag:

1 block ramen noodles
1/8 cup freeze-dried vegetables

Also take:

2 packets parmesan cheese and the ramen flavor packet to taste.

In camp: Add 1 1/2 cups boiling water to the bag and let sit for 10 minutes.
Add the flavor packet at this point, stir, then drain off most of the liquid. Toss
in the parmesan, mix well and eat.

Yield: Serves 1

Note: If you need salt after a long day, do not drain the liquid; eat it as soup.

Shrimp Ramen

In a quart freezer bag put:

1 shrimp flavored block of ramen. Tape the seasoning packet to the outside of the freezer bag.
2 Tbsp dried or freeze-dried carrots
2 Tbsp dried onions

Also bring:

1 foil pouch of shrimp
1 packet of red pepper flakes.

In camp: Add 1 1/2 cups of boiling water to the ramen and veggies. Seal and mix well by shaking and rolling, till the ramen gets soft, put in a cozy for 5-10 minutes. Put the packet of shrimp in the cozy underneath to warm it up.

Add the shrimp, the flavor packet (add to taste), stir. One can drain the noodles or eat it as a soup.

Yield: Serves 1

Simple Veggie Ramen *Vegetarian*

In a quart freezer bag put:

1 block ramen noodles (no flavor packet)
1/4 cup freeze-dried vegetables

Also bring:

1 tsp dried spices of your choice (chili powder, garlic, oregano, etc.)
1/4 - 1/2 cup parmesan cheese in a zip snack bag.

In camp: Add 1 1/2 cups boiling water to the ramen. Put in a cozy for 5-10 minutes. Drain off almost all the water, add spices and cheese, toss.

Yield: Serves 1

Pasta Primavera

In a quart freezer bag put:

1 block ramen (save flavor packet for another day)
1/4 cup freeze-dried vegetables mix

Also take a small snack baggie with:

1 tsp blend of Italian herbs, granulated garlic, salt & pepper.
1 packet of olive oil (or 1 Tbsp)

Also take:

6 packets parmesan cheese (3 Tbsp).

In camp: Add 1 1/2 cups boiling water to ramen/veggies. Put in a cozy for 5-10 minutes. Drain well, add butter, herbs and cheese, mix well.

Yield: Serves 1

Tuna Ramen & Cheese

In a quart freezer bag put:

1 package ramen noodles (save flavor packet for another day)
1/4 cup freeze-dried peas

In a sandwich bag put:

2 Tbsp cheese sauce powder
1 Tbsp dry milk
1 Tbsp butter powder

Also take:
1 pouch tuna (3 oz)

In camp: Add 1 1/2 cups near boiling water to the ramen/peas. Put the tuna pouch into the cozy with the freezer bag, then let sit for 5 minutes. Drain off remaining liquid saving about a 1/4 cup. Toss in the dry ingredient bag and enough liquid to make a sauce. Add in the tuna, stir and enjoy.

Yield: Serves 1

Thai Peanut Noodles

In a quart freezer bag put:

2 blocks ramen (no flavor pack)

At home mix in a second quart freezer bag/or container:

1/2 cup peanut butter
3 tsp spicy sesame oil
1 1/2 tsp soy sauce or tamari
1 tsp onion flakes
1/2 tsp crushed hot red pepper
2 Tbsp vinegar

In camp: Add 2 cups near boiling water to the ramen bag. Put in a cozy for 5 minutes. Add 1 cup warm water to the peanut butter bag, and stir well. Drain the ramen, and toss the noodles with the sauce.

Yield: Serves 2

Note: The sauce will carry fine for a day or two on the trail. Double bagging is a good idea.

Chicken Noodle Casserole

In a quart freezer bag put:

2/3 cup ramen noodles (break up)
1 packet cream of chicken soup (1 cup size)
1/8 cup freeze-dried peas
1 Tbsp freeze-dried mushrooms crumbled
1 tsp dried parsley
1/4 tsp granulated garlic

Also take:

1 pouch of chicken (7 oz)
1 Tbsp Italian breadcrumbs or crumbled chips.

In camp: Add the chicken and 1 1/3 cups near boiling water, stir well and put in a cozy for 10 minutes. Top with crumbs.

Yield: Serves 1-2

Ramen Stroganoff

In a quart freezer bag put:

2/3 cup ramen noodles (break up into pieces)
1 Tbsp dried onion
3 Tbsp freeze-dried mushrooms crumbled
1/4 cup dried hamburger

Also take in a small bag:

1 1/2 Tbsp sour cream powder or one packet of cream cheese
Pinch of nutmeg
Pinch of granulated garlic

In camp: Add 1 1/8 cup boiling water. Stir well and put in a cozy for 10 minutes. Add in sour cream, stir well.

Yield: Serves 1

Note: Sour cream powder can be found online. A good source is Walton Feed. Dried mushrooms can be substituted for freeze-dried ones, crumble up small to speed up hydrating time.

Chicken Ramen Stew

In a quart freezer bag put:

1 pkg. ramen noodles (no flavor packet)

In a second quart freezer bag put:

1/4 cup freeze-dried vegetables
1/4 cup freeze-dried chicken
2 packages cream of chicken soup (1 cup size)
1 tsp dry onion

In camp: Add 1 1/2 cups near boiling water to the ramen. Put in a cozy for 5 minutes, drain off any remaining water.

In the second bag, add 1 cup near boiling water, stir. Put in a cozy for 5 minutes. Toss the ramen together with the second bag.

Yield: Serves 1

Ramen Trail Spaghetti I

At home put on a dehydrator 1/4 cup dried commercial sauce (use a smooth sauce). After you dry it completely, run it thru a blender or food processor until a fine powder.

Put in a quart freezer bag:

1 package ramen noodles (no flavor packet)

In a second freezer bag put:

1/4 cup dried ground beef
Dried spaghetti sauce powder

Also take:

1/4 cup parmesan cheese

In camp: Add 1 1/2 cups near boiling water to the ramen bag. Put in a cozy for 10 minutes. Add 1/3 cup boiling water to the meat bag and stir well. Put in a cozy for 10 minutes. Drain water from the ramen, toss into the meat bag and mix well. Add in cheese to taste and enjoy.

Yield: Serves 1

Ramen Trail Spaghetti II

1 block ramen noodles crushed
2 tsp. spaghetti sauce seasoning mix
1 package tomato soup (1 cup size)
1 Tbsp dry onion
2 tsp Italian seasoning
(Optional) 1/4 cup dried ground beef

In camp: Add 1 1/2 cups near boiling water, stir well and put in a cozy for 10 minutes.

Yield: Serves 1

Wraps, Burritos and Everything Else

Wraps and burritos are one of the easiest meals on the trail. Grab whatever style of tortillas you like, and whatever you like to put inside. If you are out for a day hike, overnighter or your first night on a longer trip, we suggest you bring bags of lettuce and crunchy vegetables. That extra crunch a texture is really nice and doesn't weigh a whole lot either. To make a burrito different, try adding salad dressing instead of salsa. Here is a tip if you are a messy eater, like my husband. Bring a piece of aluminum foil about 12 inches long and as wide as the box it comes in. Then you prep your wraps on it, roll the burrito up in the foil and unravel the foil in strips as you go for "no mess" eating.

As for everything else in this section, they are recipes that didn't fit into a grouping for the book, but I still felt were worthwhile to include.

Thai Shrimp Wraps

In a quart freezer bag put:

1 cup instant rice
1 Tbsp dried onion
1 Tbsp powdered coconut cream
4 Tsp dried cilantro
1 Tsp diced dried ginger
1/2 Tsp granulated garlic

Also take:

5 oz canned/pouch shrimp
4 soft taco size tortillas

In camp: Add the drained shrimp and 1 cup near boiling water. Stir well and let sit in a cozy for 5 minutes. Make wraps with the filling.

Yield: Serves 2

Note: Swiss cheese slices are a great add-in.

Turkey Wraps

In a quart freezer bag put:

1 cup instant rice
1/4 cup toasted almonds
2 Tbsp dried onion
1 Tsp powdered ginger
2 Tsp dried cilantro
1/2 Tsp dried lemon peel. (Grate it off the lemon using a micrograter)

Also take:

4 soft taco size tortillas
1 can turkey or chicken (5 oz)

In camp: Add meat (including broth) and 1 cup near boiling water. Stir well and let sit in a cozy for 5 minutes. Make wraps with filling.

Yield: Serves 2

Note: Swiss cheese slices are a great add-in.

Hamburger Cheesy Veggie Wraps

In a quart freezer bag put:

1/4 cup dried ground hamburger
1/4 cup plus 1/8 cup instant hash browns
1/4 diced dried carrots
1/4 cup diced dried tomatoes
1 Tbsp dried onions
1 tsp dried oregano
1/2 tsp granulated garlic
2 Tbsp cheese sauce powder

Also take:

2 tortillas
Salsa packets

In camp: Add 1 1/4 cups near boiling water, stir well, and let sit in a cozy for 10 minutes. Serve on tortillas.

Yield: Serves 1

Note: By adding 1 cup of instant rice, along with 1 cup more near boiling water, it would make 4 wraps, serving 2.

Taco Couscous Burritos

At home in a mixing bowl put:

1 1/2 cups of couscous
1 packet taco seasoning mix
2 Tbsp dried onion
1 Tbsp dried bell pepper flakes

Mix up well, and divide between 3 quart freezer bags.

Take with you on your trip:

1 bag of the above mix
2 tortillas
2-4 packets salsa
cheddar cheese

In camp: Add 2/3-3/4 cup boiling water to a packet. (2/3 produces couscous tender, 3/4 would produce a saucier couscous). Stir well and put in a cozy for 5 minutes. Put cheese on tortillas, the couscous mixture and salsa. Wrap and eat!

Yield: Each packet serves 1

Bean & Rice Burritos *Vegetarian*

In a quart freezer bag:

1/2 cup instant rice
1/4 tsp granulated garlic
1 Tbsp dried onions

In a second quart freezer bag:

1/3 cup instant refried beans

Also take:

4 tortillas
2 parmesan cheese packets, or cheddar cheese
1 salsa or picante packet per burrito.

In camp: Add 1/2 cup near boiling water to the rice, and 1/2 cup to the beans. Put in a cozy for 5 minutes. The beans may be thick, add water to liking. Spread the beans on tortillas. Put rice and toppings on top.
Yield: Serves 2

Stuffing, Potatoes & Everything Else

Note: Check the FBC web site for a feature we call "Tater Tuesday" where there are new recipes using potatoes just about every Tuesday.

Thanksgiving on the Trail

In a quart freezer bag put:

1 1/2 cups instant stuffing

In a second freezer bag put:

1 packet gravy (1 cup size)

Also take:

1 teaspoon of olive oil (1 packet)
1 pouch of chicken (7 oz)

In camp: Put olive oil and 1 1/4 cups near boiling water into the stuffing bag and mix. Put chicken into gravy bag, add 1 cup near boiling water and stir. Place both bags in a cozy for 5-10 minutes. Pour the chicken over the stuffing and serve.

Yield: Serves 1-2

Taters, Ham & Cheese

In a quart freezer bag put:

1 package instant potatoes (any flavor, 2 cup water size)
1/4 cup freeze-dried corn

Also take:

7 oz foil package of ham
3 cheddar bells / 2 oz cheese

In camp: Add the ham and 2 1/4 cups near boiling water to the bag, and stir. Add the cheddar and put in a cozy for 5-10 minutes. Stir and enjoy.

Yield: Serves 1-2

Beef and Mashed Potatoes

In a quart freezer bag put:

1 package instant mashed potatoes (flavor of choice, 2 cup water size)

In a second quart freezer bag put:

1/2 cup dried hamburger

In camp: Add 1/2 cup near boiling water to the hamburger bag. Add 2 cups near boiling water to the potato bag, and stir well. Put both in the cozy for 10 minutes. Drain off any extra water from the hamburger and mix into the potatoes. This one is just rife for possibilities for you to spice up with dried items for your outdoor cooking arsenal. Maybe some dried chives, corn. How about some wasabi coated dried peas on top for a kick? Soon you will be constructing your own FBC style meals!

Yield: Serves 1-2

Unstuffed Potatoes *Vegetarian*

In a quart freezer bag put:

1 Tbsp butter powder
1/4 cup dry milk
1/2 cup instant potatoes
2 Tbsp parmesan cheese
Salt to taste
1/4 tsp granulated garlic

In a second freezer bag put:

2 Tbsp freeze-dried peas
2 Tbsp finely chopped dried carrots
1 Tbsp dried bell peppers

In camp: Add 1 cup near boiling water to the potatoes and 3/4 cup boiling water to the veggie bag. Put in a cozy for 10 minutes to simmer. Drain the vegetables and add to the potatoes. Mix well.

Yield: Serves 1

"Chicken", Stuffing and Gravy

In a quart freezer bag put:

1 cup instant stuffing mix
1 Tbsp dry onion
3 tsp. chicken gravy mix
1/2 cup Textured Vegetable Protein (TVP) chunks (smaller, the better)

In camp: Add 1 1/2 cups near boiling water and mix well. Put in a cozy for 5-10 minutes.

Yield: Serves 1

Chicken & Cranberry Gravy with Mashed Potatoes

In a quart freezer bag put:

1 cup instant mashed potatoes
1 tsp salt
1 tsp dried chives
Ground black pepper to taste

In a second freezer bag put:

1 pouch chicken gravy mix (the add 1 cup water type)
1/2 cup dried cranberries

Also take:

A pouch of chicken (7 oz)

In camp: Add 1 cup near boiling water to the potatoes, stir well. Add 1 cup near boiling water to the gravy mix, stir well and add chicken. Put in a cozy for 10 minutes. Stir again, pour over potatoes and eat!

Yield: Serves 2

Note: This is my favorite backcountry potato recipe. I first tried this recipe in the Quinault Rain Forest, sitting in a teepee shelter while rain poured outside. For me, it says spring!

Chicken, Gravy & Stuffing

In a quart freezer bag put:

1 1/2 cups instant stuffing mix

In a second quart freezer bag put:

1 packet chicken or turkey gravy (1 cup size)

Also take a pouch or can of chicken(5 - 7 oz.)

In camp: Put 1 cup near boiling water in the gravy, stir well, and add the chicken, stir and seal well. Put in a cozy. For the stuffing bag, add 3/4 cup near boiling water, stir and seal well. Put in the cozy for 10 minutes. Fluff up the stuffing, and pour the gravy over it.

Yield: Serves 1

Note: A bit on the salty side, but great after a long hot day!

Turkey & Mashed Potatoes with Gravy

In one quart bag put:

1 package of Idahoan potatoes (2 cups water size, any flavor.)

In a second quart bag:

1 packet chicken or turkey gravy mix (1 cup size).

Also take:

A can or pouch of chicken or turkey. (5-7 oz size)

In camp: Add 2 cups near boiling water to the potatoes. Add 1 cup near boiling water to the gravy. Mix well. Add the meat to the gravy. Seal well, and put in a cozy for 5-10 minutes. Pour the gravy over the potatoes.

Yield: Serves 2

Pesto Bacon Taters

In a quart freezer bag put:

3/4 cup instant hash browns
1 Tbsp crumbled freeze-dried mushrooms
1 Tbsp bell pepper flakes
1 Tbsp bacon bits

Also take in a small bag:

2 Tbsp toasted pine nuts
1 Tbsp dry pesto mix
1 Tbsp parmesan cheese (shelf stable)

Also take 1 packet olive oil (1/2 Tbsp)

In camp: Add near boiling water to cover veggies, let sit in a cozy for 10 minutes. Drain off the water, reserving about 2 tsps, dump in small bag contents and oil, and mix well.

Yield: Serves 1

Note: Dry pesto mix is found in the pasta and sauce packet aisles.

Tamale in a Bag

In a quart freezer bag put:

1/2 cup instant refried beans
1/4 cup freeze-dried corn
1 Tbsp dried onion
1 Tbsp dried bell pepper
1 Tbsp dried tomato flakes/bits

Also take, 2 packets salsa or picante sauce 1 tortilla and 1 oz of cheddar cheese.

In camp: Add 1 cup near boiling water. Stir well and put in a cozy for 10 minutes. Meanwhile tear up half the tortilla into tiny pieces and cube the cheese. Add this to the beans and stir in. Eat with the other half of the tortilla.

Yield: Serves 1

Miss-Q's Tater De-Lite

In a quart freezer bag put:

1/2 cup freeze-dried or 1 pouch of chicken
1/4 cup freeze-dried corn

In a second quart freezer bag put:

1 pouch instant mashed potatoes (2 cup water size, any flavor)
1 Tbsp butter powder
2 Tbsp dry milk
1/2 to 1 cup french fried onions

In the first bag, add 1/2 cup near boiling water to cover the chicken and corn, and let sit for a little bit to rehydrate.

In the second bag, add 2 cups near boiling water and stir well, getting all the potatoes mixed in. Add chicken and corn at this time, the extra water in the chicken/corn mixture will finish moistening the potatoes.

It will be ready to eat as soon as the potatoes and corn and chicken are completely mixed. Add salt and pepper to taste, and sprinkle on top the onions and enjoy.

Yield: Serves 2

Note: If you cannot find freeze-dried chicken, you can use canned or pouched chicken. Just subtract 1/2 cup water.

Cheezy Mashed Potatoes & Chicken

In a quart freezer bag put:

1 1/2 cups instant potatoes
1/4 tsp salt
1/3 cup instant milk
3 Tbsp cheese sauce powder

Also bring a 7 oz foil pouch of chicken

In camp: Put the pouch of chicken in the bag, and add 2 1/4 cups near boiling water. Stir well and let sit for a minute.
Yield: Serves 1

Dessert

The special dishes, that while not a top priority when you get to camp, are awfully nice to have. When you can make it simple, easy to prepare and darn tasty, it can be worth it. Some of these recipes serve more than one, so your friends will be even more endeared to you when you pull it out and can share with them.

As stated earlier in this book, not everything has to be health food when it comes to outdoor food. Does one need dessert? No, but it sure hits the spot after a long day and if it is lightweight and easy to enjoy, why not pack it in?

For the puddings in this section, a great trick is once you have added the cold water to bag and mixed it around, set the pudding in a stream if available. Just make sure it is not going to float away. For the brave, if there is snow or ice on the ground, take a one gallon zip top bag with you and put handful or two of ice or snow in. Next add cold water, two packets of salt, seal the bag and shake to mix. Now, open the bag and place the sealed bag with the pudding mix in the bigger bag. The simple chemistry of the ice, salt and water makes the pudding cool down super fast and set up quick.

Trail Ice Cream *Winter Time Only*

Ingredients needed:

1/2 cup dry milk (no soy milk)
2-3 Tbsp sugar
Pinch of salt (single use packet)
1 tsp vanilla extract, instant coffee, cocoa, banana or strawberry extract

In a quart freezer bag reconstitute 1/2 cup dry milk with 1 1/3 cups water. Shake and blend very well.

Add the other ingredients and blend very well.

Find the driest, cleanest and whitest snow you can find. Add handfuls of the snow, and stir quickly.

NOTE: Don't eat too much in the cold of this. Eating snow can lower your core body temperature.

Piggy Pudding

In a quart freezer bag put:

1 package chocolate instant pudding
2/3 cup dry milk

In separate snack bags put:

1/4 cup crushed peanuts
1/2 cup crème sandwich cookies, crumbled

Also take:

3 oz coffee liqueur
3 oz chocolate syrup

In camp: Add 1 3/4 cups of cold water to pudding mix, add liqueur, seal bag and shake well. Put crumbled cookies into individual cups, pour pudding mixture over the top, and allow it to set. Warm chocolate syrup bottle in warm water, then drizzle syrup over pudding.

Yield: Serves 2-4

Peanut Butter Cups

In first quart freezer bag put:

1/4 cup margarine
3/4 cup peanut butter

In a sandwich bag put:

3/4 cup graham cracker crumbs
1/2 pound powdered sugar

In the second quart freezer bag put:

1 1/2 cups semi-sweet chocolate chips

Also take:

A piece of heavy duty foil and make a "mold" about the size of a typical
backcountry cooking pan (think 4 cup size).

In camp: Drop the peanut butter bag into gently boiling water until it "melts".
Remove from water and mix in sugar and crumbs. Press the batter into the
bottom of your "mold". Melt chips in their bag in gently boiling water. Pour
the melted chocolate over the crust, and set aside for an hour, if you can wait
that long.

Yield: Serves 1 pig to a whole crowd.

Trail Cheesecake

In a quart bag put:

1 package no-bake cheesecake mix
2/3 cup dry milk

In camp: Add 1 1/2 cups very cold water and either start shaking or stir for at
least 3 minutes. Making sure the bag is well sealed, either chill in a stream, or
snow field for 1 or more hours.

Yield: Serves 1 pig to 4 sharing adults.

Note: This works really well on graham crackers. If you are feeling fancy, cut
one of the lower corners of the bag and squeeze out the cheesecake like you
were decorating a cake. If the cheesecake mix comes with fruit topping, now
would be the time to squeeze it on too.

Trail Pudding Pies

In a quart freezer bag put:

1 pkg Cookies & Creme instant pudding
2/3 cup dry milk

Also take:

A 6 pack mini graham pie shells
A package of small chocolate pieces.

In camp: Add 2 shy cups of water to the bag. Seal and start shaking well for a good 3 minutes. Pour into pie shells, top with candy and let set.

Yield: Serves 3 sugar addicts or 6 sharing adults.

Trail Rice Pudding

In a quart freezer bag put:

1 cup instant rice
1/4 cup dry milk
1/2 cup golden raisins
1/2 tsp cinnamon

In a second freezer bag put:

1 package instant pudding mix (small box, serves "4" size) Vanilla work well.
1/2 cup dry milk

In camp: Add 1 cup near boiling water to the rice bag. Seal and let sit for 10 minutes. In the pudding bag add 2 cups COLD water, and start shaking the well-sealed bag, making sure no powder stays in the corners. Add the rice mix to the pudding and mix well.

This is a great desert to make while dinner is "cooking". After mixing the two bags together, if you have a stream or snow bank, cool it some more so it stays thick.

This recipe can also be made smaller by halving the rice part (but keeping the pudding mix the same).

Yield: Serves 2-4 sharing adults.

Trail Pudding

In a quart freezer bag put:

1 package instant pudding mix, whatever flavor you like
1/2 cup dry milk

In camp: Add 2 cups filtered/purified really cold stream water (it needs to be cold!!), stir and seal. Holding the top, start shaking that bag good for a couple minutes-if doing in the summer and it is hot, pop the bag in the stream and let chill for 5-10 minutes or till after dinner.

Grasshopper Pudding

At home in a quart bag put:

1 package instant pistachio pudding
2/3 cup dry milk

Also take 12 mint or chocolate sandwich cookies that are smashed up. The pudding is also good with a 1/2 - 1 tsp of mint flavoring or crème de menthe added.

In camp: Add 1 3/4 cups cold water, seal, and shake/knead very well. Serve with cookie crumbles.

Yield: Serves 2-3

Pina Colada Pudding

In a quart freezer bag put:

1/4 cup diced dried pineapple
1/3 cup dry milk
1/4 cup instant coconut pudding mix

In camp: Add 1 cup cold water, seal and shake till well blended. Let the bag sit in a cold creek for 10 minutes to set.

Yield: Serves 2

Tiny Peach Pies

In a quart freezer bag put:

1/4 cup + 2 Tbsp chopped dried peaches.

In a second bag put:

1/3 cup dry milk
1/4 cup instant vanilla pudding mix
1 tsp vanilla powder
1 tsp butter powder
1/4 tsp cinnamon
Pinch of nutmeg

Also take a 4 pack of small graham cracker crusts

In camp: Add 1 cup near boiling water to the peaches. Let sit for 10 minutes, then cool in a stream. Add in the second bag, and stir well. Let cool in the stream for 5-10 minutes more. Serve in the pie crusts.

Yield: Serves 2-4

Trail Pudding Pecan Pies

In a quart freezer bag put:

1 package butterscotch instant pudding
2/3 cup dry milk

Also take:
A 6 pack of tiny pie shells, you can substitute tiny graham cracker shells.
1 package crumbled pecans.

In camp: Add 1 1/2 cups cold water to the pudding and shake very well, kneading the bag for about two minutes. If possible, store the pudding in a stream or river till dessert time (make with dinner). When ready, divide between the shells, and top with pecans.

Yield: Serves 3-6

About the Author

Sarah has been hiking since she was a child and backpacking since she was in college in the early 1990's. She is a cofounder of a regional hiking group, the Pacific North West Hikers. Her favorite outdoor activities include; hiking, backpacking, car camping and snowshoeing. Her favorite area to hike and backpack is Mt. Rainier National Park in Washington State.

Sarah is a Washington State native and currently lives in the foothills of Mt. Rainier with her husband, son and two overly indulged white cats.

She can be found on the web these days at www.freezerbagcooking.com or www.traildivas.com.

She can be contacted at sarah@freezerbagcooking.com.

Index

Almonds 49, 50
Apples 25, 28
Bacon 23, 82
Banana 14
Beef 55, 78
Burritos 76
Cabbage 25, 28
Cappuccino 17
Carrots 5, 27, 29
Cashews 48
Chai 19
Cheese 40, 69
Cheese Sauce 47, 60, 81
Cheesecake 85
Chicken 36, 39, 40, 41, 44, 47, 48, 49, 50, 51, 52, 53, 56, 57, 70, 72, 79, 80, 81
Chicken Bouillon 36, 49, 53, 57, 62, 64
Chowder 31, 32, 33, 34
Coffee 17, 18, 20
Cole Slaw 26
Corn 28
Couscous 3, 6, 10, 12, 36, 38, 39, 59, 60, 61, 62, 63, 64, 76
Cozy 2
Cranberries 44, 80
Curry 28, 35, 49, 50, 54, 56, 61
Eggnog 17
Gravy 79, 80
Green Beans 29
Grits 13, 58
Ham 77
Hamburger 44, 45, 71, 75
Hummus 40
Ice Cream 84
Low Sodium 6, 21, 51, 53, 54, 55, 57, 60, 64
Mocha 18, 20
Mushrooms 5, 58, 62
Oatmeal 11, 12

Onions 5
Parmesan Cheese 67
Peaches 88
Peanuts 70
Peanut Butter 14, 41, 85
Pecans 88
Pie 86, 88
Pilaf 60
Pina Colada 87
Pineapple 24
Pork 54
Potatoes 14, 31, 32, 78
    Mashed 6, 31, 32, 33, 78, 80, 81
Pudding 84, 86, 87, 88
Raisin 27
Ramen 11, 35, 38, 66, 67, 68, 69, 70, 71, 72
Rice 6, 10, 35, 36, 43, 44, 45, 46, 47, 48, 49, 50, 51, 52, 53, 54, 55, 56, 57, 58, 76
    Brown 51, 52
Rice Pudding 86
Salad 23, 24, 25, 26, 27, 38, 39, 41
Salmon 32, 58, 60
Shake 16, 84
Shrimp 68, 74
Smoothie, 21
Soup 35, 36
Spaghetti 71, 72
Spinach 38, 45, 47, 52, 63
Stuffing 79
Sushi 34
Tamale 82
Tomatoes 5, 39, 62
Tuna 63
Turkey 74
Vegan 54, 63
Vegetarian 34, 54, 57, 63, 68, 76, 78
Wraps 13, 14, 39, 40, 41, 73, 74, 75
Zucchini 25

Made in the USA
Lexington, KY
30 June 2013